You are the Master of
your destiny!

Your Blueprint, Life by Design

This book is available at special quantity discounts for bulk purchase for sales promotions, premiums, fund-raising, and educational needs. For details email Roland@RolandByrd.com.

ISBN 978-1-45648-933-5

Book Cover Design By Vauna Byrd

Contents

This book is dedicated to my wife, Vauna.
Vauna, there are no words to express my gratitude and thanks for your support, love, and belief in my ability to change. You have been the light in my darkness, the compass constantly guiding me home, and my inspiration to grow into someone I'd never imagined I could become.

I would also like to recognize and thank all of my children.
I want you to know that I am prouder of you than any father could ever hope to be. Thank you for loving me and believing in me. I continually strive to become the father you deserve.

Endorsements

"Your Blueprint offers a fresh, unique perspective about your Subconscious Beliefs, the Law of Attraction, Personal Accountability, and how they intermingle to create your life." - Joe Vitale, as seen in the smash hit movie, "The Secret."
www.mrfire.com

"What a wonderful thing you have done to help others have the tools to change their lives for good! ...I really enjoy your style. It's like I'm talking with you." -
Cathy Baker

"I had the great privilege of being asked by Roland to review his manuscript. I was blown away with the depth with which he explores the different facets that make up our life's blueprint. Even more valuable is his ability to design exercises that prize open long held non serving beliefs, and delivering our personal way forward. This book gives you the state of play and a solid game plan to make the right moves for you." -Richard Cartmer-Edwards. Founder
www.Heroes4Change.com

Foreword

Roland Byrd could easily have been dead and never written this book. I hope that got your attention because if you're like me, you usually skip the foreword, wanting to get straight into what the author has to say. Who cares what the author's friend has to say in the foreword? Well, you should know two things before skipping the forward: (1) I've never met Roland Byrd. (2) And this is the first forward I've ever accepted the invitation to write.

Additionally, you might like to know 6 things before reading this book (or not reading because you were about to overlook its power).

1. This is a VERY exceptional book, perhaps it is even a great book. (And I've read hundreds of self-help books over the last 20 years).
2. This book was forged from the fires of Roland Byrd's personal challenges which almost left him dead.
3. This book rose from the ashes of Roland's inspiring, relentless and authentic desire and determination to make good of himself and his life. That it exists is proof in and of itself that the advice in the book works.
4. Mr. Byrd, with this his first book, has shot up a flare indicating that he has the chops to become widely known as the next great self-help author.
5. This book is the epic and astute guide for how to turn around your life and achieve success, fulfillment, happiness and prosperity.

But this book isn't perfect. It does have one major weakness. This book fails to tell you who Roland Byrd is really, what he's come through, and how he operates outside of the pages of this book. And that's what my foreword is for.

First of all, Roland buried his difficult upbringing and depression well into half-way through the book, an act he is easily forgiven for. Perhaps he doesn't yet understand how helpful it is for the reader to know how much he's survived. Or perhaps he hasn't fully come to terms with it yet himself. Nonetheless, you deserve to know sooner that Roland Byrd has overcome a lot. At one point in time his marriage was collapsing, he was a brooding depressed father who felt like "a waste of flesh." He was suicidal. And all of this surely took root when as a child he suffered physical beatings at his own step-father's hand. Roland had a personal challenge, and he turned his life around using the wisdom he's sharing in this book.

Again, I've never met him. Roland came to know me through my personal development company. He's one of our associates. But we've never met. The only reason I know Roland is because he began writing me letters about 8 or 9 months ago. Very personal letters, typed and single spaced, each from two to five pages long. And again, these were very personal letters. In each, Roland would tell me about his personal development journey, of his latest thoughts on improving himself and his life, of his self-discoveries. Of his breakthroughs. Of his successes. And even of his failures.

Now, to get one single letter in this day and age is unusual to say the least. And for that letter to be long, and thoughtful and inspiring is even more uncommon. I can count on one hand how many people have written me a letter like that in the last 18 years of my being a public persona. But Roland wrote me such a letter. And then the next week another letter. And the next week another letter. And another and another and another. For whatever reason, Roland has written me enough letters in the last 8 or 9 months to stuff full a decent sized box. And through these letters I've come to know how truly dedicated, intelligent, wise and authentic Roland Byrd is around the topic of changing one's life to become a better person with a greater life. He's changed his own life and he's a man on a mission to help change as many other people's lives as possible.

I told you there were 6 reasons you should read this book.

6. You should read this book because Roland Byrd is the real deal. He's turned his own life around by living and breathing what he writes about. By pulling himself out of a painful past that would have swamped most other people. By acting from the depths of his soul on his better judgment to heal his life and all those in need whom he can reach.

As a transformational guide, inspirational speaker and success coach of 17 years now, and having personally interviewed more than 150 of the Best of Best in the world for their results in money, health, relationship, business, sports, happiness and spirituality, I can truly tell you that this book is chalk full of damn great advice, a complete success system, and is extraordinarily thorough and insanely insightful. I promise you this book tells you exactly how to succeed massively, even if you're down and out when you begin. This book holds its own against every success manual I've ever read.

Like Roland, I know anyone can better their life based on the will to do, the courage to try it, and the know-how provided in this epic book.

Burn Bright,

Patrick Combs
June 22, 2010
Flying somewhere between Denver and Baltimore.

My Catalyst for Change

I believe in living a life that is constantly moving forward, a life that is flexible, dynamic, and fluid. I believe past errors and failures are valuable lessons for growth and progress. Even so, there are life-lessons where the price is too high, where the lessons could and should have been learned another way. But I'll come back to that in a moment.

I used to have a different set of beliefs...

In the past I believed I was the victim of my life. I used things that happened to me in my childhood, and throughout my life, as excuses for choices I was making. I told myself "Rational Lies" to justify my behaviors.

I did some horrible things, things that I am ashamed of, that fill me with remorse, and that, if I were to focus on them, would crush me with regret and sadness.

Let me tell you briefly about one of those lessons. Without question it is the one part of my life that I would change if I had the power to do so. I would give anything to take back the pain and damage I caused.

But I can't. And that's a tough pill to swallow.

Nothing *I ever do* will undo my past choices or the harm they caused others. I've had to learn to accept that. Otherwise, I'd flounder through the rest of my life in a haze of despair birthed from remorse and regret. And while some people might be happy to see me in that place, it wouldn't serve my family—because I wouldn't be the man I am today—and it wouldn't serve you—because I'd never have learned the lessons that I'm passing on in Your Blueprint. These lessons, if you let them, will create marvelous changes in your life.

So...what was the lesson that caused such dramatic change in my life?

Read on.

In December 2007 I found out that the police were investigating me for questionable text messages I'd sent to a 15 year old young woman I knew. That same day I confessed my actions, regarding this young woman, to my wife and my church leaders. A few days later I met with the police and confessed to them.

Then my life entered a limbo of sorts. My wife and I separated. I moved out of my house and, *determined to never repeat that kind of behavior*, I immediately began to get counseling. Six months later charges were pressed. I turned myself in and pled guilty to sexually abusing the young woman. This was not a plea-bargain. The only caveat I had from the prosecutor was that if my psycho-sexual evaluation came back as low-risk to re-offend, they would recommend probation instead of prison.

In September of 2008 I was sentenced to Felony Probation and ordered to register as a sex-offender.

(The prior few paragraphs are the only mention of my crime you'll find in this book.)

The easy path would be for me to hide my head in the sand, live a small life, and avoid any publicity. That's not who I've become though. I've learned powerful methods to change my psychological, spiritual, and emotional blueprints.

Let me ask you a question, "Knowing what I know now, living a new life, having changed myself and my life so dramatically, *how could I keep these processes to myself?*"

Would you hoard your knowledge if you knew it could help others change their lives for good?

Of course not!

You'd shout it from the hilltop! You'd help as many people as you possibly could!

That's what I'm doing. It's one form of restitution for me.

The true beginning of my transformation, the miracle that started my path of healing and change was the spiritual rope my wife tossed me in December, 2007. As you'll discover later in *Your Blueprint, Life by Design*, she offered me a glimpse of hope, that there might be a way for me to change who I'd become. I clung to that hope with all my might. It became the foundation for my psychological, spiritual, and emotional changes that followed.

Since December 2007, I've been a dedicated student of personal development. It became my mission to rewire my mind, to learn everything I could to become the man I can be instead of the man I was. This is why I've studied the power of the subconscious mind. I'm fascinated by it.

It's my mission to learn everything I can to empower myself to make healthy and proactive choices, choices that keep me in places of psychological, spiritual, and emotional safety and to make sure I never allow myself to hurt or abuse another person.

I continually seek ways to grow, change, and improve myself. I've devoured many books and courses on personal development. I strive daily to live the lessons I've learned. Sure, I'm not perfect at it, but I always seek to improve and become a better person.

My desire to help others and share the knowledge I've gained is a natural outgrowth of the path I've chosen. After all, knowledge gained is wasted if you don't use it and share it with others!

I also feel that sharing the knowledge I've gained is a small thing I can do to give something back.

I am gladly serving my probation and continually striving to improve myself and to empower others, to help them discover the miraculous power that is already within them.

And if even one person is able to change the course of their life as a result of the lessons in *Your Blueprint, Life by Design*, then all of the effort, passion, and love that I put into these pages is well spent.

I invite you to visit the *Break the Silence Foundation USA* website. Break The Silence USA is designed to eradicate all forms of sexual abuse through education. *Awareness is the first step to lasting change.*

http://www.BreakTheSilenceUSA.org

Thank you

Roland

One last thing: If you suspect that anyone you know is being sexually abused or sexually abusing another. Please report it to your local authorities! *It's better to do something and be wrong than to have been right and do nothing.*
We must all stand together to end sexual abuse!

Introduction

Since you're reading this book I'm going to imagine there's something you're ready to change about yourself or your life. I don't know what it is. You might not know what it is. You might know exactly what you must change. Or perhaps you just have a nagging feeling that *"Something's Gotta Change!"*

Whichever of these applies to you, it's alright. You're in the right place!

Did you know your Subconscious Beliefs are largely responsible for the results you get in life?

It's True!

These beliefs are *Your Blueprint.* Think of them as the autopilot that engages when you aren't consciously controlling your life—which is most of the time. Better yet, imagine a burly co-pilot who insists on going a different direction than you want. You can fight and fight your co-pilot, but he's a lot stronger than you (80% to 90% stronger) and in the end you'll lose the battle.

Right now you might think, "Great! So I'm not in control of my life! It's my subconscious that's running the show..."

Pause for a moment because there's great news! You can *reprogram Your Blueprint!*

Where force fails, you can talk sense into your subconscious mind. Realize that your subconscious doesn't necessarily listen to reason; it deals with feelings and beliefs. But once you learn to speak its language *You'll convince it that what you want is best.* Then your subconscious mind will put all its considerable power and energy into getting you where you want to go. That means the burly co-pilot will change course and fly toward the destination of your dreams instead of the destination he wanted.

Cast aside your old beliefs and behavioral patterns that came from living life as the victim of your history. *Program your subconscious mind with new, empowering beliefs and behavioral patterns.* Start becoming the person you always knew you could be! Start creating the life you desire!

Once your subconscious understands that what you want and what it wants are the same, you'll fly to heights of joy, happiness, and success you've only imagined before!

Rewrite Your Blueprint and in a short time you'll realize the results you're getting from life are aligning with your goals and dreams!

Why?

For the first time in your life your subconscious mind is working for you because your subconscious beliefs align with your desires!

Become one of the heroes of your life.

The greatest thing about being human is the ability to take charge of our lives. Accept accountability today. Realize that, though your subconscious beliefs steer your life, *you control those beliefs*.

Use **Your Blueprint, Life by Design** as the platform to *burst free of your cocoon, realize your true inner power, take control of your life,* and *accept the amazing person you are!*

Take control of your life today! Make the choice, change *Your Blueprint* and change your life!

You are the master of your Destiny!

Roland

Your Blueprint

Your Blueprint consists of all your subconscious beliefs. *Your Blueprint* is the rule book your subconscious mind uses to decide how to interpret and interact with people and events in your life. The beliefs that make *Your Blueprint* can be empowering, crippling, or in-between. And while it is possible for people to have subconscious beliefs that run the gambit, there usually is a common theme. That's why people tend to be either positive or negative in how they view life.

When something happens that contradicts *Your Blueprint*, your subconscious mind experiences the discomfort of dueling realities. Then it immediately starts working to bring the world back in line with what it believes reality should be. This creates a comfort zone because your subconscious mind needs to know that your beliefs are valid. Whether they are true or not is irrelevant. The subconscious mind accepts them as fact and must find a way to validate them.

An example of this is people who win the lottery only to go bankrupt in a few years. Their Blueprint "rules" of being poor are challenged by the wealth they now have. So their subconscious mind sets about finding a way to get rid of the money! Once the money is gone, their subconscious mind is again comfortable with what the physical world is telling them about their reality.

Mission accomplished!

This is also why some people never have lasting relationships. If their Blueprint says that being in a relationship ultimately means pain, they will subconsciously sabotage their relationships when they start to feel vulnerable. This proves to them that relationships do mean pain, which validates their Blueprint. Then they have "subconscious permission" to leave the relationship before the pain becomes more than they can handle.

In some cases people unintentionally develop new subconscious beliefs. Something happens and they experience a paradigm shift that allows them to believe in their new reality. Sometimes this means they had great pain about their old reality; enough pain to drive their subconscious mind through the discomfort of forging and accepting new beliefs. Sometimes it happens through inspiration; suddenly they realize a better way is possible. In either case, they have then rewritten a section of their Blueprint. When this happens, their subconscious mind fights every bit as hard to bring their new reality to pass. *It begins working for them*.

Your Blueprint is a lot like the magnetic polarity of your life. In the following illustration, a magnet is surrounded by metal shavings. These shavings represent the undesirable habits and situations in your life.

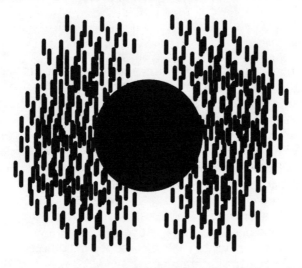

Most people will "do something" to force these undesirable things away from them. They take some action that changes their circumstance without changing their Blueprint. If it's weight, they'll go on a diet. If it's lack of money, they might get two jobs.

These actions take care of the symptoms *as long as there is force applied to keep them from returning.* But they do not affect the core beliefs that *cause* the symptoms. They do not change their Blueprint.

When a force is applied to keep the symptoms at bay, the magnet and shavings look like this.

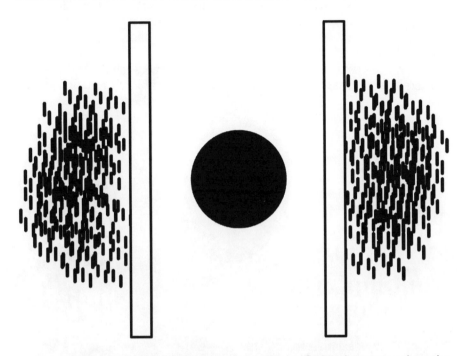

When their Blueprint hasn't been altered, what happens when the barriers between them and the undesirable things are removed?
Right!
Because the magnetic core hasn't been altered, the shavings come rushing back.

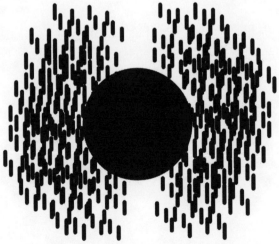

The only way to make a lasting change in your life is to demagnetize yourself. To do this, you must change your subconscious beliefs. Only then will you stop attracting those undesirable things into your life! You must *Rewrite Your Blueprint*!

Once that's done, what happens to the metal shavings when the barriers are removed?

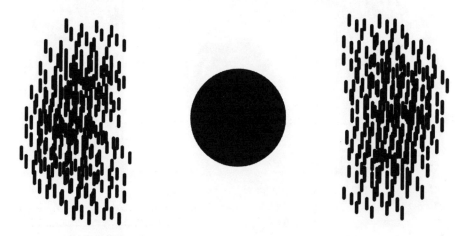

The undesirable things stay where they are, because you are no longer attracting them into your life with a flawed Blueprint!

Knowing this, you can *intentionally* change *Your Blueprint* and then harness the power of your subconscious mind to create the life you desire.

Next we'll discover the power of choice...

Key Points

> ➤ ***Subconscious beliefs*** form the lens through which you view the World. The way you view the World is your reality. Your subconscious mind works constantly to bring your surroundings and your life in line with these beliefs. As a whole, all of your subconscious beliefs form the Blueprint for your life.

> ➤ ***Your Blueprint*** is like the root system of the tree that is your life. If you don't like the fruit that your tree is producing, it does little good to throw away the fruit and hope for better results without tending to the health of the tree as a whole. Start with the roots. If the roots are rotten, the tree will fail. It might even die. If the roots are healthy and strong, the tree can survive many things and will eventually produce healthy fruit.

> ➤ ***Change Your Blueprint*** *and you change your subconscious mind's reality. This causes your subconscious mind to strive mightily to find a way to make your life fit its new beliefs.*

The Power of Choice

Life is choice. The way you interpret reality is a choice. The meaning, the reality that you perceive in life, is completely up to you. Something good, or bad, can come from any situation. The only difference between whether something positively or negatively impacts your life is the meaning you choose to give it.

What are you going to *choose* to do?

Try asking yourself these questions.

- What meaning do I *choose* to give things today?
- When something I don't like happens, do I find the good in it?
- When something I do like happens, do I express gratitude?
- When something I don't like happens, do I express gratitude for the ability to learn and grow from it?

Think about your answers. They might just give you extra insight as you read on.

Perception *is Personal Reality*

Everything is neutral until you give it meaning. And everything that happens contains equal amounts of positive and negative. Much, if not all, of the meaning you give things comes from the part of the situation you focus on. Do you focus on how the situation can help you or how it can harm you? That largely determines what the impact, and meaning, of the situation will be to you.

Epictetus said, "Men are disturbed, not by the things that happen, but by their opinion of the things that happen."

Think about this: Have you ever seen a community, church, or country come together to help others after a natural disaster? Or a nation step in and defend a weaker country from an aggressor? What about situations like the civil war and massacre in Rwanda where no one really stepped in but massive, positive impact has touched the world in the years following the atrocity? The more catastrophic or horrible a situation, the more *good can come from it.* The key is that in situations like these, people have to be willing to look for the good to find it.

In Chinese cosmology Yin and Yang represent two opposite but equal forces in nature that combine to produce all that comes to be. Yin is the feminine, passive principle and is exhibited in darkness, cold, or wetness. Yang is the masculine active principle and is exhibited in light, heat, or dryness. Neither Yin nor Yang is good or bad, those are meanings we apply to them. One cannot exist without the other; and nothing exists that isn't an equal combination of the two. As long as something exists, there are two halves to it.

Think of it mathematically, any number greater than zero can always be divided by two and give you a result that is greater than zero. You can also divide any positive number by two infinitely without ever reaching zero. So, as you realize, everything has two parts, two halves to it. Which half are you going to focus on, the half that helps you or the half that hinders you?

It's up to you. But I know what I choose!

So...how do you view the world?

What meaning do you give the everyday things that happen in your life? Are you optimistic and positive in most things? If so great! If you're not, that's ok too. Either way you've just made the choice to notice how you're filtering things. Not only is this the first step in changing or improving your process—because you won't change something if you don't know it's a problem—but it's a huge step toward growing into the person you want to be.

Challenge:
I challenge you to find the positive in everything! For the next thirty days make it a point to deliberately look for the positive in everything that_happens in your life. And I mean EVERYTHING!

After thirty days of consciously looking for the positive in all things, you'll be well on your way to creating a life-long habit of optimism.

Here's a short story to show how I apply this in my life.

Today I was moving a piece of exercise equipment that I own. I noticed slight resistance as I lifted the top half. I looked up to see what it was...right as the light fixture above me shattered. I could have been upset that I broke the light fixture or that I wasn't paying attention or that now I needed to buy a new fixture or that I needed to clean up glass or vacuum the floor. Yadda, yadda, yadda. Instead the first thing I thought was how wonderful it was that no glass got on me, or in my eyes, and then I thought how glad I was that it was an easy fixture to replace.

I never got upset or even thought to come down on myself. The best part is that I've made this type of positive thinking a habit. I didn't have to consciously choose to find the positive in the situation; it's what I've trained my brain to do. So I found it without trying.

That seems easy with something relatively small, like the situation I mentioned above. But what about traumatic or life changing events; how do you find the positive in them?

First, realize the only difference between a traumatic, life-shattering event and one that creates new purpose and meaning in your life is how you interpret it. That's right; *the responsibility for how events affect you is yours*. Whether or not you care to admit it, it is a choice. If you've experienced something traumatic, what meaning did you give it? Did that meaning help you or hinder you? Now that you know you have a choice, what meaning will you choose to give that experience? Are you going to let these events shatter your world or *create a new, crystalline purpose for your future?*

Second, realize that the best way to prepare yourself to find the positive in traumatic situations is to create a habit of finding the positive in little, everyday things. When you're used to looking for the positive, it will be natural to look for it in all situations, big or small—this is why I challenge you to look for the good in everything that happens over the next thirty days.

This doesn't mean that you shouldn't experience normal emotions like grief or sadness as a result of some things. What it means is that you accept these things and look for the positive side too. When you create something meaningful from hardship or pain, you'll also heal faster emotionally and physically.

Looking for the positive in all situations increases emotional flexibility and reduces stress. When discovering the positive in situations is your habit, happiness will be your companion. Finding the positive in situations is a choice. All choices have consequences. In this case, the consequence of looking to the positive side is helpful; it improves the quality of your life.

Think about how you feel when you hear the word "consequence". Doesn't "consequence" have a negative feel? That's because "consequence" is usually used to describe punishment, or other undesired results, that happened to someone because of something they—or someone else—did. This is another example of perception creating reality. Merriam-Webster's 2 most common definitions for Consequence are: *1 : a conclusion derived through logic : INFERENCE and 2 : something produced by a cause or necessarily following from a set of conditions.* So, in reality a consequence is just a result or conclusion. It is neither positive nor negative...*Until we apply meaning to it.*

Another interesting thing about perception is how people tend to filter the behavior of others. Pay attention to what you think and feel when you see someone do something. Think of the meaning you apply to their actions (and words). If you really examine it, you'll discover that what you think they mean matches what you would mean if it were you performing the action or saying those words. Your mental filter gives their action your meaning. The action or words may, or may not, have that meaning to them, but you interpret them as if they did. In other words, we filter other's actions through our own view of reality. And then to complicate it further, they filter our actions through their view of reality. It's like trying to drive around Chicago with a map of NYC while you listen to someone give directions in a foreign language!

And we wonder why so many people have trouble communicating!

This might feel strange at first, but it's worth it. When you find yourself filtering others behaviors, take a mental step back, or pause your thoughts and ask yourself, "Am I judging their behavior from my autobiography?" Realize that they might not mean what you think they mean. This will help you learn to take actions at their face value.

For example, if you're having a conversation and the other person looks away, it simply means that they looked away. That is a fact. Any meaning as to "why they looked away" is your applied meaning, or assumption, about what their action meant.

With people I have rapport with; I find it helpful to ask them what they meant when they did or said something. The answers are often far removed from what I thought they meant.

Challenge:
I challenge you to take things at face value! For the next thirty days make it a point to realize that other's actions might not mean what you think. When you need clarification, ask. And when you realize that someone else is filtering your actions, ask them what they think you meant or said. Then clarify what you meant if needed.

When you take things at face value—and ask for clarification as needed—it will improve your relationships, both professional and personal. This habit allows you to communicate more clearly and helps prevent misunderstanding.

It is my belief that most misunderstandings people find themselves in are the result of mismatched communication filters—which is another way of saying the communication beliefs of their Blueprint.

As an example I'll share a story of an interesting conversation my wife and I had a little while back:

My wife and I were at my mom's house. Now, my mom lives in a place where air conditioners aren't considered a necessity because it doesn't get very hot in the summer. But there are days when one would be nice. It was around 85 F outside that day, but it felt a lot warmer in the house. In hopes of cooling things down, my wife opened the living room windows and shades to get air circulating through the house.

A bit later we started a movie for the children. I watched it from the kitchen and noticed a glare on the TV. So I went over and dropped the living room shades.

A few seconds later my wife asked me, "Do you think it's warmer outside than it is inside?"

At first I had no idea why she asked me that question. But we've been married awhile, so it finally hit me and I said, "Do you think I closed the blinds because I didn't want the air to circulate? I closed them because of the glare." Then I went over and opened them to let the air back in.

I went back into the kitchen and—wanting to prove my point about the glare—I said, "I can see the neighbor's porch perfectly!" (Of course I should have said "reflected in the TV.")

My wife replied, "I've never seen anyone between the houses." I really wondered what in the world that had to do with the image of the neighbor's porch on the TV...

"What does that have to do with the glare?" I asked

"I thought you meant you wanted the blinds closed so the neighbors couldn't see in the house." She said.

We both laughed about this whole exchange. But it demonstrates how much our perception of events control our view of reality. Think about the facts of the situation. She opened the windows and the blinds. There was a glare on the TV. I closed the blinds. There was less air flow in the house. I opened the blinds again. There was a glare on the TV. Everything else was exclusively the result of our individual interpretations of the events.

Next we'll explore the connection between Choice and Accountability.

Key Points
> ***Things are neutral*** until you give them meaning.
  o Choose the meaning that helps you succeed and grow.
> ***There are equal amounts*** of good and bad in every situation.
  o Find the good and you'll attract more into your life.
> ***We filter other's actions*** based on our meaning.
  o Take things at face value.
  o Ask what they meant and seek clarification. You'll reach a new level of understanding and your ability to communicate will soar!

Choice and Accountability

When it comes to choice and accountability popular media would have us believe that people, and their lives, are controlled by reaction and causality. We are bombarded with messages that people do things, not because they choose to, but because some external force puts them in a situation where "they have to do it".

Movies and television shows portray infidelity as glamorous; rich people are portrayed as conniving and manipulative. First-person shooter video games desensitize our children to shooting people—because our minds can't tell the difference between a real experience and one that is vividly imagined. Crime is justified and criminals made the heroes in many films, books, and TV shows. Situational integrity is taught as the norm. Additionally most stories reported on the local and national news revolve around tragedy or mishap.

Think about the message you're sending your subconscious mind when you choose to fill your free time with these things. What you get from life is the direct outgrowth of what you think, feel, and do. What you do is influenced by how you feel. How you feel is influenced by what you think. What you think is shaped by what you absorb mentally and what you focus on. What you absorb mentally is largely controlled by the choices you make about what to watch, listen to, and read.

Do you see the pattern? If you want to be happier and more optimistic about life, then choose to fill your mind with happier and more optimistic things! After all, if you want to grow healthier plants in your garden would you pour battery acid on them?

I think not!

Now I'm not saying that all movies, TV shows, and books are like battery acid to your brain. After all, *there are* many great things to watch, read, and listen to. But if you don't like the results life is giving you, you might take a moment to analyze what you're filling your head with.

Yeah, I know...DUH!

Or is it?

Take a look and see what you find, because as you now realize, the way you use your "spare time" has a great impact on the shape of your life.

Challenge:
I challenge you to pay close attention to the messages you're feeding your subconscious mind! For the next thirty days think about the thoughts, feelings, and moods the things you read, watch, and listen to create. Ask yourself if the messages you're taking in are ones you really want. If they aren't, then change the things you're doing.

Remember, a path that heads downhill will never reach the mountain's peak.

When you decide to fill your mind with positive things, you'll find that your outlook on life will soon follow. And changing your outlook is key to creating the life you desire.

Next we'll cover the true meaning of success...

Key Points
> **The things you feed your subconscious mind** affect your perception of life.
   o Stack the deck in your favor by feeding your subconscious positive and uplifting things. You will find your outlook on life turning more positive. And *you will attract better things into your life!*

Just What Is Success?

What is your definition of success? Take a moment and write it down here.

_____

_____

_____

_____

_____

_____

_____

_____

_____

_____

_____

_____

_____

_____

_____

_____

_____

_____

_____

_____

_____

_____

_____

There are no right or wrong answers to this question. Though there are some that make more sense than others. Some people find success in the ability to do things well. Others consider themselves successful if they have good relationships with friends and family. And some consider themselves successful if they have lots of money.

But there is always a common element to true success. *True success NEVER harms others!* This is paramount to becoming truly successful. No matter what your personal definition of success, you must *never hurt others* in the process. If you are doing things right now that damage others, you must *stop that behavior* and figure out how to help others instead. Only then will you begin to experience actual and lasting success.

One of the major areas of success in life can come from your career. Because your career can also have tremendous impact on your personal life, you should choose it carefully.

If your work is unfulfilling, you'll often bring negative emotions home with you. This hurts you and the people in your life. Also, if you despise your job, how can it inspire you to reach your true potential? If your career is a chore, you know that you'll have no passion for it! Work is just that, WORK! To me that's one of the worst four letter words!

But when you love your career, you'll be excited to go to work, you'll want to stay up on the latest trends, and you'll love learning new ways that you can grow and excel in your field. Dare I say it? You might even *have fun!*

When you have passion for your career, you'll naturally find ways to help others succeed with you. And you'll bring positive emotions home after a rewarding day! This helps the loved ones in your life, because it not only creates a healthier atmosphere at home; it also inspires them by showing that a *career can be fun and rewarding!*

A successful career often leads to financial success as well. And while this type of success alone doesn't make a person truly successful, it helps pave the way to true success in life. Because if you're successful in your chosen line of work, you'll have an easy time building the financial base you need to live the life you desire; and to help others!

The next diagram shows the three major components necessary to enjoy a successful career. (Diagram based on "The Three Steps To Success", pg 139 *The Power of Your Subconscious Mind*—Joseph Murphey, Ph.D., D.D.)

Following these steps will put you well on your way to *personal and career success.*

1. Discover your passion.
2. Specialize in a line of work that feeds your passion and strive to excel in it.
3. Be certain that your passion contributes to the success of others as well as your own.

Answer these questions and you'll discover how each of these pieces builds on the one preceding it.

How can you ensure that your passion contributes to the success of others, as well as your own, until you've chosen a line of work that uses and feeds your passion?

How can you specialize in a line of work that feeds your passion, and strive to excel in it, if you haven't discovered your passion?

To discover your passion download the *Discover Your Passion* Report at:

http://www.YourNewBlueprint.com/bookbonuses

Challenge:
I challenge you to discover your passion! Once you know what your passion is, start taking steps toward it. If your passion is in a different career, you needn't change careers today but you should start moving toward it today.

Personal success is a combination of all other types of success.

- Career
- Financial
- Relationships
- Spiritual

True success comes from succeeding in all of these areas. Only then you will have the highest level of personal success.

Remember though, that the true measure of your success is in the quality of your life in each of these areas. Only you can measure the quality of your life. You must *live up to your standards*. You are the only person who can say where your life should lead. And you are the only one who can walk the path before you.

"Success is measured by your discipline and your inner peace." — Mike Ditka

"Your time is limited, so don't waste it living someone else's life." —Steve Jobs

For me to be successful I believe I must:

- Learn to be great at what I do.
- Empower others as much as I can.
  - By sharing the wealth and knowledge God has blessed me with.
- Have good relationships.
- Be financially independent.
- Make a dent in the universe.

- Enjoy life and live every day to the fullest.

The thing about success is that it's a path, not a destination. Like life, success is in the doing. You can be successful every day. At first you might not look successful to the world and those around you. But, aside from that not mattering in the least, as you live each successful day, you'll create a more successful tomorrow.

Success breeds success because like attracts like.

With that in mind, one of the best ways to become successful is to find someone who is doing what you want to do and *Model Them!*

If you have to model this person from afar, that's ok. But if you can find someone who is willing to get to know you and share their knowledge directly, you'll be amazed at how quickly you start to excel. This is partly because we unconsciously raise or lower our personal vibrations (our energy level that influences the world around us) to match the vibrations of those we interact with. A person who is succeeding at high levels is on a totally different vibrational level than someone who isn't. Just being around a truly successful person will help you become more successful because you will raise your vibrations to meet theirs. Or at least to get as close to theirs as you can.

For example, have you ever done something with a group of people who were better than you? Chances are you performed better than normal. This isn't coincidence. You know they are better. You pay attention to what they are doing. You mimic them, at least subconsciously. You see them do something you didn't know was possible and suddenly you think, "I can do that!"

That ignites the desire to improve. And soon you find you're doing things that you hadn't thought you could. You elevate your performance subconsciously because your mind is opened to new possibilities.

This is exactly what modeling is about. You don't need to reinvent the wheel. Someone already invented it! So if you want to make a wheel, go find a person who knows how and *Learn From Them!*

The other part of modeling is being a mentor. This is just as important as finding someone you can model.

I think of it as the circle of responsible modeling.

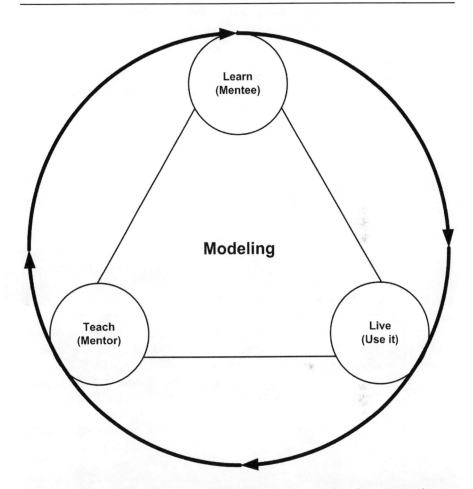

We model someone to improve ourselves and to learn new things. In doing this, we become the mentee. We use what we've learned in life, which helps us become more successful in some way. Then we take the knowledge we've received and use it to help others grow by mentoring them.

A teacher is always a student and a student is always a teacher. This method keeps you from becoming stagnant. It ensures you'll continue to grow and I believe it shows God, and the universe, that you are a responsible steward of the knowledge that you've been given.

If a pool of water becomes separated from a stream it will quickly turn foul and dry up. If water is added to the pool it will regain some of its life. But real vibrancy comes when the pool is joined again to the stream and water freely transfers between the two.

This is how our intelligence works. We learn best when we continue to *seek* new knowledge *and share* what we've learned.

Challenge:
I challenge you to model someone! Find a mentor and learn from them. Now take the knowledge you're gaining and share it with others. Become a river of knowledge.

You'll be astounded at how quickly you learn new things when you're willing to implement and share what you learn.

Now that you know your definition of success, you might wonder what success sounds like...

Key Points
  - ➢ **Discover your Passion**
    - o Passion for your career will help you achieve your financial goals, have a better home life, and help others succeed!
  - ➢ **True success helps others**
    - o Success is a road, not a destination. As you help others along the way you'll realize even greater levels of personal achievement!
  - ➢ **Model successful people**
    - o When you share the knowledge you gain, you'll learn faster and have lasting results.

The Language of Success

The language you use without thinking is the language of your true Blueprint. The way you speak is directly related to your ability to succeed, because the things you say and the way you say them directly affect your emotional state and your beliefs. And, in many ways, your subconscious is like a child. Unless the things you tell it directly conflict something it believes, it has no reason to doubt you. If you say, "I can't afford that." Your subconscious mind says, "Alright," and makes sure something happens so you'll never afford it. *But* if you say, "I'm going to buy that," (which is a statement your subconscious mind can believe because of the open ended time frame) your subconscious mind will start working to make that reality.

The same is true of all the things you say to yourself.

Here is an example of how negative self-talk and language use has limited one man's ability to succeed.

The other day a very smart man I know said to me, "I'm just slow. I've always been slow."

I was dumbfounded by his statement because I'd seen him do things that obviously—to me—required a great deal of intelligence. "Why do you think you're slow?" I asked.

"It's just the way I am." He said and shrugged. "When people tell me things, I don't catch on for a day or two. And most of my bosses take advantage of me because they know I won't catch on until it's too late."

"I think you're really smart." I said. "Do you think that maybe being slow is just your belief..."

"No," he interrupted me emphatically, "I'm slow. I have been all of my life."

Wow! His belief in his "slowness" was so strong, that the very mention of an alternative sent him into instant defense.

We talked for a few more minutes. Everything he said was steeped in failure. "I can't this. I'll never afford it... This is just the way my life is. I can't ever make enough to pay my bills..."

I shifted tack and told him, "I believe in you." And that, "I know you are smart enough to make the changes you need to in your life." He seemed to be listening, until I asked him to write out a goal highlighting where he wanted to be financially next June. Then the failure voices in his head kicked into overdrive.

I could almost see the conversation he was having in his head. His shoulders slumped. His expression fell. He looked as if someone were berating him for daring to think he might change.

This is how that portion of the conversation went.

"I'd like you to write a short goal about where you want to be financially next June." I said. "Date the top June 9th or so and write something simple like: I'm so happy and grateful now that I receive enough money every month to easily meet all of my family's wants and needs. And that you're grateful for the income producing activities that were provided which allowed you to reach this goal."

"OK. I can do that." He said.

"I'd like you to do it tonight." I said. "It will only take five minutes."

"I can't do it tonight. I've got too much to do." He shrugged again and looked at the floor. "I'll do it tomorrow."

"It will only take you five minutes." I encouraged him.

"I just don't have time tonight." He went on, "I can't do it until tomorrow."

"OK." I said. And this time I shrugged.

This type of negative language and self-talk creates a self-defeating cycle. The person believes they cannot succeed and they see evidence of their failure to succeed. They notice the evidence of failure and comment on it internally and to others. Talking about their evidence of failure reinforces their internal beliefs that they cannot succeed.

And round and round it goes!

This cycle shows how when people's Blueprint tells them something is true, they will subconsciously find evidence to reinforce their "truth" everywhere. It also reinforces the fact that until someone genuinely wants to change—and that means their desire to change is greater than their fear of change—there is little hope of them changing.

Notice also that a major part of this cycle is the language that's used. Then ask yourself, "How many times a day do I say, 'I can't'?"

But what about happy successful people, what language do they use in their internal and external communication?

Easy. Happy, successful people use Happy, Successful Language!

This is a phone conversation I had with my six year old son, Ethan, this morning.

"Hi Dad, how are you?" Ethan asked me.

"I'm great, Ethan. How are you? Are you great too?"

He thought for a moment, "Yes. I am. Dad, I hope you have a great day!"

"Thank you, Ethan. I will. I hope you have an awesome day too!" I said.

"I will, Dad." Ethan said, and then said something that touched me deeply. "Dad, I just want you to know how proud I am of you. And that I'll always love you no matter what!"

I grinned from ear to ear, "Thank you, Ethan. I hope you know that I'm very proud of you too! I'm proud of who you are and who you're becoming. And I love you too!"

"I know Dad." He said. "I have to go now. Bye" And he was off doing the things that are important to a six year old.

This conversation is similar to those I have with all of my children. Everything they say is usually packed full of optimism, love, and joy.

And yes. They do misbehave at times.

Maybe you're wondering why I'm using a six year old as an example of someone who is happy and successful. Because he is! Ethan believes in himself. He believes in being happy and finding joy and love in the world. He believes that his needs will always be met. He believes that he can do anything he sets his mind to. To me those are signs of a successful person—regardless of their age. And, his language shows this is true.

Successful beliefs are natural to children. It's only when we "well intentioned adults" try to protect our children by imposing our limiting beliefs on them that they lose their successful beliefs. After all, why should they doubt us?

Remember, you have no idea what you are truly capable of—well, you might be getting an idea by now. And you have no idea what your children or others whom you love are truly capable of. Please allow them to grow into the magnificent, creative, successful people that they were designed to be!

In other words; be careful what you say because not only are your beliefs showing, they are likely shaping the beliefs of those around you...

I want you to think of someone you know who is happy, optimistic, and successful. Remember conversations you've had with them. Think of the words they used. Think of the imagery they used and they way they spoke. Pay attention to the facial expressions they used during your conversation and their body language. Did they convey excitement? Did they lift you emotionally during the conversation? Were you happy that you spoke to them?

People who are *genuinely happy and optimistic* are infectious. This is why people who want to be happier radiate toward them. And people generally like them. Being likeable helps your ability to succeed. When people like you, they want to help you and to be around you. When you use language that positively affects yourself, you are using language that positively affects those around you too. Your language creates a bubble of radiated optimism and happiness and that draws others to you.

Check yourself. This list contains positive – empowering – phrases and negative – disempowering – phrases.

Positive	Negative
I can...	I can't...
I'm learning to...	I'll never be able to...
I'll figure it out...	It won't work...
It doesn't have to be that way...	That's just the way it is...
What can I do differently?	What did I do wrong?
How does this help me?	Why did this happen?

Which ones do you use most throughout the day?

Challenge:
I challenge you to pay attention to the language you use in all your communication! For the next thirty days, anytime you catch yourself saying something that is disempowering or self defeating; change it to an empowering phrase like the positive phrases listed above.

You'll be amazed at how much your outlook on life improves with this one simple change.
Now ask yourself, "Do I speak the language of success?"
Well, do you?

Next we'll cover the impact your focus has on your success...

Key Points:

> ➤ ***The language you use*** without thinking shows the true state of *Your Blueprint.*
> ➤ ***Successful people*** use successful language.
> ➤ ***Start using happy***, optimistic, successful language and you'll be much closer to the realization of your dreams and desires!

Focus and Success

As Maxwell Maltz revealed in his 1960 classic, *Psycho-Cybernetics*, every human has a built in goal-seeking success-mechanism. This mechanism is more wonderful and accurate than that of any other creature on Earth. And, of all the creatures on Earth, humans are the only ones who *can consciously program their success-mechanism*.

This success-mechanism works automatically. This makes it easier to operate and program than any machine. Because of its ability to function automatically, most people don't realize it's there. They use it every day, they program it every day with random bits of information, and they don't even know it!

Imagine how a computer program would function if it were programmed that way? It wouldn't even work. And yet, this is how most people program their success-mechanisms, and thereby their lives!

So, if humans have a built in success-mechanism, why are so many people unsuccessful? The success-mechanism isn't controlled by judgments about good and bad, right and wrong, or wealth and poverty. Your success-mechanism automatically reacts to the target coordinates you feed it every day. It neutrally accepts its directive and diligently seeks the goal. It is perfectly impersonal. It simply doesn't care whether its target will have a positive or negative impact on your life. The only thing it's designed to do is find a way to reach its target destination. And it does that with incredible accuracy!

Your success-mechanism seeks goals that match the rules defined in *Your Blueprint*. It's guided by subconscious beliefs that you developed throughout your life. These beliefs were formed through interaction with those you care for and by what you focus on every day. Even the things you take in, or pay attention to, without realizing it leave an imprint.

For example, my oldest son, Ethan is turning six years old. He is still in a very impressionable phase of his life. A few months ago he was acting up while I talked to my wife on the phone. I asked what was going on and she said, "He's just having issues today."

Ethan overheard this. Over the next few days, when he would do something he wasn't supposed to, he would say, "I can't help it, it's my issues!" And he really believed that he had no control of what he was doing.

Over the next few weeks his behavior became increasingly disruptive and with every incident, he would blame his issues.

Once I realized what was happening, I found an opportunity to talk to him when he was acting up. He was so upset that he was shaking and crying and he told me that he couldn't help it because of his issues.

I took his shoulders gently and looked him right in the eyes. "Ethan," I said, "You do not have any issues. What you have are choices. Sometimes, when you make a poor choice you have consequences that you don't like. But these *are choices* and consequences, not issues." Our conversation was a little longer than that, but that's basically it.

Then I assured him that I loved him and had him repeat to me his understanding of what I'd told him. I gave him a big hug and sent him on his way. From that point on, he has never blamed anything on his issues.

So, as you know, when he overheard that he was "having issues" he believed it. His subconscious mind took it as a "valid reason" for his behavior and started to build on it. When I broke his pattern and told him that he had no issues, he believed me—this is key—and then his subconscious mind accepted that new belief as the reality and "his issues" disappeared.

The tone of *Your Blueprint* affects the way you interpret reality. If you have a negative outlook on life, you have a negative belief system in *Your Blueprint*. If you *have a positive outlook on life*, you have a positive belief system in *Your Blueprint*.

Certainly you know someone who finds the negative in any situation. They love to talk about how bad things are and seem to have the "worst luck". They could even win $10,000.00 and find negatives in the situation. They might complain about the taxes or how long it takes to get the money. Things like that.

And you probably know someone who is the polar opposite; someone who can *find the positive in anything*! This person could lose their job, and *turn it into a winning scenario*.

Why is that?

What causes such dramatic differences in the way life events are interpreted?

People only see what they look for; they only notice the things that align with the rules of their Blueprint. *You only see what you look for.* And the more you notice something—positive or negative—the more of it you'll find. Because by looking for it, by noticing it, you're giving it attention. Attention equals focus and focus creates reality.

The image on the next page is half light and half dark. Imagine that the dark half represents negative things and the light half represents positive things.

Focus on the dark half first. Study it intently and draw the page closer to you until the dark half fills your field of vision. Then look at the next page where it is entirely dark.

By focusing on only the dark half, it has become the only thing you can see!

Go to the next page and repeat the process by studying the light half of the image, drawing it closer until it fills your field of view and then look at the next page where it is entirely light.

Roland Byrd

This time, the light half of the page is the only thing you see. *Because it is your focus!*

As you know, by focusing on only the dark or the light, you reach a point where it becomes the only thing you can see. Unless you drastically change your focus, the focal point becomes your reality. But both halves, the light and dark, *are still there!*

This is true of this exercise and of life.

What do you want your reality to be? Are you 100% happy and satisfied with your life?

If not, keep reading and change your focus. If so, I'd wager you're already a student of life and are always seeking to expand your knowledge. In either case, you attracted this book because it has much more information in it that will prove invaluable to you.

Next we'll discover what makes up your success-mechanism...

Key Points
- ➢ **We all have a built in success-mechanism** that we can learn to use to our advantage.
- ➢ **Your success-mechanism seeks goals** that match the rules (subconscious beliefs) outlined in *Your Blueprint.*
  - o If you don't like the results you're getting in life, change the rules of *Your Blueprint.*
- ➢ **Your Focus Determines** your *Reality.*
  - o If you aren't happy with your reality, change your focus.

The Three Major Components

Of

Your Success-Mechanism

(The Law of Attraction
The Reticular Activating System
&
Your Subconscious Beliefs)

The Law of Attraction

The Law of Attraction states: *Whatever you give your time, energy, and focus to you attract into your life.*

Whole philosophies of personal development hinge on this single law of the Universe. And rightfully so! There is nothing better than learning to *deliberately attract* what you desire into your life. If you desire more love, give more love, show gratitude for the love you receive, notice all the love around you. If you desire more money, start by noticing the money you have. Show gratitude for it. Celebrate all the money you receive, even the pennies you find on the ground. And most of all; learn to *feel the abundance* that already exists in your life.

Another way to interpret the Law of Attraction is this: whatever you give to life is what you'll get from it. If you give kindness, you'll receive kindness. If you are generous with others, you will receive more generosity. Some people call this Karma. Some people say it's God's way of giving us what we deserve—good or bad—from life. Whatever your thoughts are, the reality is that The Law of Attraction is working in your life every moment.

The Law of Attraction is mentioned in many spiritual and wise texts.

TAO chapter 23 "...One who devotes himself to Virtue is one with that Virtue; And one who devotes himself to losing is one with that loss. To the one who is with Virtue, the Way also gives Virtue; While for the one who is one with his loss, the Way also disregards him." (Translated from the Ma-wang-tui Texts by Robert G. Henrick. Page 76 'LAO-TZU TE-TAO CHING')

Proverbs 11:27 "He that diligently seeketh good procureth favour; but he that seeketh mischief, it shall come unto him."

Matthew 7:7,8 "Ask, and it shall be given you; seek, and ye shall find; knock, and it shall be opened unto you.
"For every one that asketh receiveth; and he that seeketh findeth; and to him that knocketh it shall be opened."

Matthew 9:29 "Then touched he their eyes, saying, According to your faith be it unto you."

Enos 1:15 "...Whatsoever thing you ye shall ask in faith, believing that ye shall receive in the name of Christ, ye shall receive it."

But the Law of Attraction doesn't care what higher power you believe in; or if you believe in one at all. It is a law of the Universe just as certain as gravity is. Do you think gravity cares if you believe in it? Take animals, they don't know what gravity is, but they're still bound by it.

As Leslie Householder, Author of the best selling "Jackrabbit Factor" states, "You cannot break a law; you can only break yourself against it." (Hidden Treasures: Heaven's Astonishing Help with Your Money Matters, Leslie Householder, pg 8.)

I've found that to be great advice. So, the sooner you accept the influence of the Law of Attraction in your life, the better off you'll be.

Many people only think of The Law of Attraction as a way to improve their financial situation. That's a great way to use it. But it is so much more! The truth is; it works for everything in your life. Simply place *positive focus* on what you want and you'll attract more of it.

When I first learned about the Law of Attraction, I thought, "If it can be used to attract financial gain and wealth, then can't it be used to attract psychological, spiritual, and emotional change too?"

Instead of only using the Law of Attraction to attract things, people, or situations in my life; I thought, "I can use the Law of Attraction to attract the ideal me!" I then experimented by setting goals for myself that involved dramatic changes to the way I'd dealt with life and how I viewed my personal reality. And guess what?

It worked great!

In fact, using the Law of Attraction this way worked so well, that it has become a mainstay in my quest for personal excellence and success!

Maxwell Maltz recounts how some mental patients were able to improve their mental health through imagination (*and the Law of Attraction— added by Roland Byrd).

> "Just Imagine You're Sane
> "San Francisco. Some mental patients can improve their lot and perhaps shorten their stay in hospitals just by imagining they are normal, two psychologists with the Veterans Administration reported.
> "Dr. Harry M. Grayson and Dr. Leonard B. Olinger told the American Psychological Assn. they tried the idea on 45 men hospitalized as neuropsychiatrics.
> "The patients were first given the usual personality test. Then they were asked flatly to take the test a second time and answer the questions as they would if they were 'a typical, well-adjusted person on the outside.'
> "Three fourths of them turned in improved test performances and some of the changes for the better were dramatic, the psychologists reported."
> "In order for these patients to answer the questions 'as a typical, well-adjusted person' would answer, they had to imagine how a typical well-adjusted person would act. They had to imagine themselves in the role of a well-adjusted person. And this in itself was enough to cause them to begin 'acting like' and 'feeling like' a well-adjusted person." (Psycho-Cybernetics, Maxwell Maltz pg 38-39)

There is another reason that this method produced remarkable results in the mental health of the individuals tested. By imagining how a normal, well-adjusted person would act, they were using time, energy, and imagination to "*focus on*" and in effect "*be more*" of what a normal person would be. Without realizing it, they were using the Law of Attraction to create healthier mental processes.

This is also called acting "As if". This is the basic concept: when you desire something in your life, start acting as if it were reality. If you have a difficult co-worker and you want to have a good relationship with them, imagine how you would act if that healthy relationship were already there. Then start behaving that way. If you want to be the number one salesperson in your company, imagine how you would act if that were already true and *start acting that way*.

You get the idea.

The Law of Attraction can attract your "ideal you". It will attract anything you show it—through time, energy, and focus—that you want into your life. So you might as well use it deliberately to attract what you desire, *because it's working in your life anyway.*

Three steps to effectively use The Law of Attraction:

- Decide what you want.
- Focus on what you want *with strong positive emotion.*
- *Move Your Feet!*

Decide what you want.

The Law of Attraction works whether or not you know what you want. With that in mind, it makes sense that the first step in *attracting what you want* is to *know what that is*. Otherwise you're just attracting whatever happens to hold your attention at the moment—good or bad. My brother, Robert, calls this, "Shiny Object Disorder." That's where something only holds your attention until you notice the next interesting (or shiny) thing. Then your attention immediately switches to the new object. This is like a two year old in a toy store. And, as you know, it isn't an effective way to attract anything of real value into your life.

So, ask yourself, "Do I know what I want?"

Realize that many people fail to achieve their goals because they don't have a clear target. They don't know what they want. If they set goals at all, they resemble these; "I want to be rich.", "I want a great relationship." Or "I want a better life." And while these might seem like good goals, they're nebulous and have no real power.

A weak or poorly-defined goal is like trying to cross the ocean in a ship with no captain, rudder, propellers, or even sails. You're at the mercy of the ocean and the elements. If you reach land, it's pure luck. And the odds of reaching your destination are infinitesimal!

But when you have a clearly defined goal, you take the same ship and outfit it with the best captain, rudder, propellers or sails, and crew. When that's the case, you'll not only reach your desired destination, but do it in record time!

The Law of Attraction works just like that ship. You *are* the captain of your life. Only you can decide exactly where you want to go. Then, and only then, can you effectively plot your course. Having *clarity of desire* helps you navigate. It acts as the rudder and power source that propel you toward your goal.

Remember, when you set goals use as much detail as you can and review them often. Doing these things place focus on your desire and will amaze you with their effectiveness.

We'll come back to goal setting later.

Focus on what you want with strong positive emotion.

When working with The Law of Attraction, positive emotion is one of your greatest allies. You know the Law of Attraction *always* brings you more of what you focus on. Feelings like love, gratitude, happiness, and abundance place you in an empowered and positive receptive state. Powerful emotions also produce powerful vibrations. Remember, positive emotions raise your vibrations and negative emotions lower them. And because the Law of Attraction responds to your vibrations, the massive shift in vibration—created by powerful emotions—causes the Law of Attraction to work overtime. Thus, you attract more of whatever produced those powerful emotions. Keep that in mind and choose to pay attention to your feelings at all times. Make the decision now to control your emotions instead of letting them control you. The proactive state this creates allows you to choose how to navigate your life.

Take your mind off autopilot.
And
Banish disempowering thoughts.

Your thoughts are the seeds you sow for your life and future. Thoughts lead to emotions. When you choose how you react to your thoughts, you more easily control the emotions you experience. This learned, deliberate control of thought allows you to experience positive, empowering emotions most of the time. And, as you know, this helps you attract more of what you want in all areas of life.

The following technique is called the "Cognitive Thinking Process". This process uses a series of questions and actions which help you evaluate and deal with disempowering thoughts. It also takes your mind off of autopilot. And not only is that an important step in taking control of your life, it's a huge step toward achieving your personal success.

I am especially passionate about this technique because I spent most of my life dealing with mild to severe depression. When I learned of, and started using, this technique--two years ago as I write this--it was as if sunlight shone into the once darkened rooms of my mind. My depression vanished almost overnight. And though I still feel sad from time to time, in appropriate situations, I've never gone back into a depression.

I also implore you, if you are experiencing depression; please consult a licensed professional to help you as my advice is not intended to take the place of professional assistance.

The Cognitive Thinking Process:

When any disempowering or negative thought comes into your mind, apply the following rules to it:

1. Ask yourself, "Is it true?" (Is this reality or imagined?)
    a. Refuse to deal with any thought until you know whether it is true.
        i. If you aren't sure if it is true then either throw it away or go find the truth.

2. If it is true, then ask yourself, "Whose problem is it?"
   a. Whoever can make a decision to fix the problem owns it.
      i. If you can fix it, own it.
      ii. If you can't do anything about it, then throw it away or give it to the person who owns it.
3. If it is true and you own it, then ask yourself, "Am I doing my best?"
   a. If you are doing your best then keep doing that.
   b. If you aren't doing your best, then figure out what else you need to do and do it.
   c. Only you and God (or your higher power) can know if you are doing your best.

Challenge:
For the next thirty days, disengage your mental autopilot. When you notice you are experiencing feelings of angst, anger, apprehension, sadness, depression, jealousy, etc. apply this process. Determine what thought or thoughts triggered the feeling and then run it through the Cognitive Thinking Steps. Do this consistently for 30 days and you'll develop a new proactive pattern that helps filter out disempowering thoughts.

When banishing disempowering thoughts becomes a habit, you'll find yourself in a much healthier emotional state than ever before. And you'll find the path of your life carrying you ever closer to your dreams.

Move Your Feet!

You can clearly know what you want. You can focus on it constantly. You can be passionate about it too. But the magic bullet is this; you still have to *Move Your Feet!* If you don't know how to start, look around for someone who's done something similar and follow their lead. Make a plan; even a simple one will get you moving. And *START MOVING!* Then follow what your gut tells you. When you receive inspiration about something, take action. The more action you take and the more persistent you are, the more quickly you will get results!

Clarity + Focus + Passion + *Persistent Action* **= Manifest Results**

Think about it this way.

You can know exactly what you want in life. You can feel highly passionate about it. But if you don't move your feet, what then? Maybe you're sitting just fifteen feet from the thing you desire most in life and you don't even know it? Unless you get up and walk around a little, you'll probably never get it!

Oh sure, someone might happen along and bring it to you. But do you really want to bank on that?

I wouldn't!

As you learn to use the Law of Attraction you'll feel insight, urges, promptings, flashes of brilliance—call them what you will. Learn to trust these feelings and *take action immediately.* Many things are time sensitive. And once an opportunity is gone, it might never come back.

That doesn't seem fair does it? But when the Law of Attraction offers you something and you tell it, "No Thanks!" by ignoring those feelings, it believes you. And it withdraws the gift.

Likewise, when The Law of Attraction brings you something you desire—even if it's only part of what you want—celebrate it. Be grateful. Notice the things you appreciate and what you like about the Law of Attraction's gift. This tells The Law of Attraction, "This is what I want!" and it will bring you more of what you celebrated.

But once you attract it, how do you keep it?

By making sure your subconscious knows what you've attracted is a good thing. Include it in *Your Blueprint!* We'll cover how to do that later.

Next we'll discuss your mind's tireless sentry...

*Additional resources for the Law of Attraction:
"Awakening The Movie" Hosted by Patrick Combs
"The Jackrabbit Factor" By Leslie Householder
"The Attractor Factor" By Dr. Joe Vitale
"Law of Attraction Book" By Michael Losier

Key Points:

> **The Law of Attraction**--*whatever you give your time, energy, and focus to you attract into your life*--is a constant law of the Universe. You can accept it. You can fight it. You can say its hogwash...
>   o But I suggest you harness it because, whether you like it or not, *it is working in your life*.

The Reticular Activating System

Radiating from your brain stem is a small network of cells, about four inches in length, called the "reticular activating system" (RAS). The RAS is the gate keeper to your mind. It determines what sensory input is important and makes it into your brain and what is unimportant and gets discarded. The more you notice something—positive or negative—the more you give it attention. Giving something attention places focus on it. This is how you program your RAS that what you've noticed is important. As soon as it learns that something is important, your RAS will start seeking and noticing more of the same. If you combine powerful emotion with what you notice, your RAS locks it in faster as a high priority item. More emotion equals greater importance equals heightened sensitivity to those same stimuli.

An example would be when you bought a new car. Do you remember how once you decided on the type of car you wanted, you started seeing them everywhere! You might have never noticed those other cars before. But once your RAS tagged them as important, you realized that they *Were Everywhere*.

When you deliberately add powerful, positive emotion to the things you desire, your RAS will shift your focus to include them in your awareness. And the more you notice them, the higher your RAS places them in its list of "things to look for." This creates a self-perpetuating cycle, gives your success-mechanism a target, and directs The Law of Attraction to bring you more of what you desire.

Now that you know how to use the RAS to attract more of what you want, I'm going to let you in on a secret. You can use your RAS to filter out things you want to remove from your life too. Simply make the choice to ignore disempowering thoughts or events, or to focus only on the positive side of events and let the negative side go. This lets your RAS know that these things are "unimportant". Once it learns that something is unimportant, it will work to filter it from your perception.

Get your subconscious mind working for you. Create the focus you want and you're miles ahead, because then you have a silent ally helping you notice the positive things. The positive things you notice are waypoints on your journey to success. They help you stay on course as you move toward your desires.

So, how do your subconscious beliefs tie into the mix?

Key Points
> *The Reticular Activating System (RAS)* controls the information that makes it into your brain and filters out the noise. Deliberately focusing on the things you desire, with powerful positive emotion, programs the RAS to notice things that help you achieve your goals. When you notice things that bring you closer to your desire, The Law of Attraction works harder to bring your desire to you.

Subconscious Beliefs

I've covered a lot of the ways your subconscious beliefs interact with the Law of Attraction and your success-mechanism. To summarize them; your subconscious beliefs form *Your Blueprint. Your Blueprint* is the rulebook that tells your subconscious how to interpret life. The way you interpret life shows in your personal vibrations. When *Your Blueprint* contains empowering successful beliefs, your personal vibrations are higher and you attract more of what you desire.

The subconscious beliefs of *Your Blueprint* also guide your success-mechanism by giving it coordinates at which to aim.

Next we'll discover the Pillars that make *Your Blueprint...*

Key Points:
> ➤ ***Subconscious beliefs*** form *Your Blueprint.* They control your personal vibrations, which affects what the Law of Attraction brings into your life. *Your Blueprint* also provides targets to your success-mechanism. When these targets are in line with your true desires, your success-mechanism will guide you toward your life dreams.
> ➤ ***When you use*** *The Law of Attraction, your RAS, and your Subconscious mind together, you utilize your success-mechanism to its fullest.* And by doing that, you will achieve things you've only dreamed of before!

The Seven Pillars

Of

Your Blueprint

Your Blueprint has seven major components. Each of these pieces works with the others to make you the person you are. They are the support pillars of your life. It's vital that you address each of them during the creation of *Your Blueprint*. If you don't, it will reduce the effectiveness of *Your Blueprint* and weaken the structure of your life.

The first pillar of *Your Blueprint* is...

Character

These are the mental and ethical traits that define you. They are what set you apart from others. Character is how you deal with life and how you treat others. Your Character shows in the way you live your life and the choices you make. Do you follow what you say all the time? Or do you only live how you should to meet others expectations?

A person's true character often shows when they are under the greatest pressure. How do you behave when things are tough? Do you treat those around you with kindness? Do you leave your ethics on the floor?

Another sign of true character is how a person acts when they think no one is watching. Do your actions in private match your words in public?

Only you know the answers to these questions. But remember, just as character can be damaged, it can be healed. A person whose character is flawed can make the choices and take the steps necessary to fix it.

Your character also affects the way the other six Pillars of *Your Blueprint* interact with each other.

For example, a person who is mean-spirited in character communicates harshly with others; they will have a dark tendency with their emotions; their finances will be affected and, even if they are financially well off, they will have no joy from it; their mental state will be affected—a mean-spirited person knows no true happiness; their physical state will be affected because they will be tight and guarded, this can lead to poor health as their bodies try to get rid of emotionally created toxins; their spiritual state will be effected because a mean-spirited person cannot truly open themselves to a loving higher power.

So, as you know, your character has great impact on your life and on your ability to make a positive difference in the world. This is why Character is one of the seven pillars of *Your Blueprint.*

Communication

Communication is integral to function in any society. The things you say, and the way you say them, directly impact how others relate to you. This includes your non-verbal communication, which can often be more important to the meaning of your message than your words.

We live in an age of ideas. The ability to relate your ideas to others is key to your success. What is it that makes you unique? What is it about your plan or idea that will help others *and* make money?

You may have the greatest idea in history, but without the ability to communicate it to those who will help you put it in motion, it may never be realized.

To be truly successful in life, you must help others as others must help you. This requires the ability to create and nurture relationships. As you know, communication is important to develop and maintain healthy relationships. Whether personal or business in nature, successful relationships *require* good communication.

The ability to communicate your value to others is also important, as is your ability to tell others of their value. This works best when you use actions as well as words. This type of communication also shows your character.

Your emotional state, mental health, spiritual state, and your character are communicated through your actions and words. Your physical state is communicated through the health of your body and the way you carry yourself. Your spiritual state is also communicated by your body.

This is why Communication is one of the seven pillars of *Your Blueprint.*

Emotion

Your emotional state directly influences your personal vibrations. These vibrations either attract or repel the things you desire. A person with a negative emotional state can never be truly successful, because their negative vibrations repel the things they think they want and attract what they are in true harmony with.

You do not attract what you want. You attract what you are in harmony with.

Knowing this, you can change your emotional state so it works for you.

A person with a negative emotional state can change it. They can start by changing their focus—from the things that worry them to the things they desire. They can also focus on feelings of love, joy, gratitude, and similar emotions. This changes their state and creates positive vibrations, which attracts more of what they want.

Your emotional state also manifests in your communication. A person with a negative emotional state is prone to complaining and dismal conversation. A person with a positive emotional state tends to focus on opportunity, blessings, and the good things that are happening in our world. Negative communication repels those who are positive while positive communication attracts them.

Your emotional state affects all areas of *Your Blueprint*. A negative emotional state is effectively the foundation for a negative life. The negative person might have success in one or two areas, but they will never truly be successful or happy.

These are the reasons Emotions are one of the seven pillars of *Your Blueprint*.

Finance

Money is a necessary part of life. It allows you to have the comforts and necessities of living. In many ways money is the lubricant that helps your life run smoothly. Without money you can't support yourself or a family. Without money you cannot help others. As long as you're worried about money, you can't become rich, because "money worry" creates negative vibrations and drives away the financial abundance that *is waiting for you*.

But money itself isn't enough. You need to be able to manage your money. Without good financial management, it is possible for a person who makes a lot of money to be poor. Many "rich" people live month to month. That's not true wealth. True financial wealth comes from creating a layer of wealth that is invisible to the world at large. This wealth should be invested in iron-clad investments and be accessible.

The best way to increase your wealth is to do something that helps others. Discover your passion. Then use it to help the world.

Remember, money is neither good nor evil. It just is. Money is a tool and once it's recognized as such, it's easier to obtain.

The way you use your money says a lot about you and ties in with the other six pillars of *Your Blueprint* in many subtle ways. This and the fact that money is needed to function in society and to help others is the reason it is one of the seven pillars of *Your Blueprint.*

Mind

The state of your mind directly impacts your perception of reality. A healthy mind sees facts as facts and opinions as opinions. It separates assumptions from facts and makes decisions based on research and knowledge instead of emotional triggers.

The mind, and the perception of reality it controls, dictates emotional responses. An unhealthy mind often battles terra-cotta soldiers. These soldiers are hollow threats and can only damage a person when they fight them. The emotional responses to these false threats create negative emotional states and thereby vibrations—which drive away the positive things that are desired.

When a healthy mind deals in facts and gathers knowledge, it is easy to maintain the positive mental state needed to attract ones desires.

Unhealthy mental states can be treated. As long as it doesn't defy the laws of nature, the mind can overcome any mental problem when there is desire and faith.

Mental state is manifest through the way one communicates and the emotions they feel. A person with an unhealthy mental state will not communicate effectively—this includes how they interpret things others say to them. They will also experience emotional responses that are disproportionate to situations. But a person with a healthy mental state will communicate well and react rationally and appropriately to most situations.

Mental state also affects physical health as the worried mind will create physical manifestation of its fears to prove them valid. Spiritual health is suspect as well when the mind is unhealthy. A person with flawed thinking has difficulty seeing the truth in things.

Truth and enlightenment are key pieces of spirituality; they cannot be explored without clear and rational thought.

These are the reasons your Mind is a key pillar in *Your Blueprint.*

Physical

Your body houses your mind and your spirit. You might refer to your spirit as your essence or your soul. But regardless of what you call it, it's the part of you that gives you your unique identity and allows you to touch the spiritual plane and be affected by it.

Your body is more than a house for your spirit though. It's a conduit between your mind and the physical realm. The five senses are the minds way of using your body to receive information about reality.

Your body is affected by and also affects your emotions. Your body posture and language will show how you feel, and by showing, reinforce those feelings. This can be helpful when you realize that choosing to use your body properly lifts your spirits and raises your vibrations.

It doesn't matter if your body is perfect. It only matters that you take care of and strive to improve your body. A person with a physically handicapped body can have wonderful physical health, while a person with a physically perfect body can have horrible health. Much of this health is controlled by the mind, as mind and body are intricately linked.

Use your body well and wisely, and it will serve you for the entire path of your life. Use your body harshly and mistreat it, and your path might be cut short.

Your body allows you to enjoy, experience, and interact with life.

This is why it is one of the seven pillars of *Your Blueprint*.

Spiritual

Your spirit is the true essence of your being. It's the unseen component that animates your body and allows you to interact with both the physical and spiritual realms. Your spirit receives inspiration through your subconscious mind, it allows you to "sense" those you love, even at great distances, and it binds you to the Infinite Intelligence that connects all humankind.

Your spirit also allows you to communicate with God or your higher power.

It is through this communication that many universal laws are fulfilled.

Your spirit is fed with love, gratitude, and joy. Happiness is its natural state. A person with a healthy spirit radiates warmth and light and attracts others with the same characteristics, just as a person with a sick or dark spirit will attract others with the same inclination.

Your spirit affects all aspects of your life and is the underlying support structure for every pillar of *Your Blueprint*. It is truly the root system to your tree of life. Feed it well and you will prosper in all things.

Next you'll discover why you should use a Personal Blueprint and not just traditional goals...

Why Not Just Use Traditional Goals?

Your new Blueprint is the ultimate design for your life. It specifies exactly who you want to become. It's not typical of most goals because it includes all the traits you need to create, and live, the life of your dreams. You might even think of it as your personal mission statement and value map; or the plan to ignite your life's passion.

All things in your life grow from the traits you design in your new Blueprint. So, I'm sure you realize, your new Blueprint must be created and tended with loving care.

The purpose of your new Blueprint is to help you become the person you want to be. Becoming this person is a process that also helps you achieve your other life goals. Think of it as reverse engineering. Instead of creating individual goals that "hopefully align" with the path you want from life; you create the *ultimate destination* for your life first. Then the proper goals to reach this destination will become apparent.

Once you've figured out what you really want from life and crafted *Your Blueprint* correctly; reviewing *Your Blueprint* will ignite the fires of possibility within you! It will inspire you! The changes and opportunities it brings into your life will continually amaze you. Reading it will fill you with feelings of joy and gratitude like you've rarely experienced before.

But why tackle such a grand design? Is it really necessary? Why not just create a few goals that take care of the things that are most important to you right now? After all, you can worry about the rest later—when it becomes important, right?

If you do it that way, it's like trying to build something without the directions. What would happen if someone dumped all of the pieces of a car on your front lawn, without tools or directions, and told you to put them together? And when I say all the pieces, I'm not talking about pre-assembled components. I mean all of the nuts and bolts and pieces of plastic and metal...all loose.

How much luck do you think you'd have putting that car together? And, if you were able to somehow assemble it, what would be the time commitment?

That's what managing your life through a string of sub-goals is like. You may or may not ever achieve your true potential!

But when you create a master design first, you're creating the Blueprint that ensures the finished product matches what you want, it fits your design. Once you've done that, you can, and should, create sub-goals when you're inspired to. Because then, inspiration for sub-goals will come to you when those goals serve you best. That's when they help you most along the path toward your true destination.

Creating your new Blueprint also helps with what I call *Knowing "your why."*

Knowing "your why" means figuring out the real reasons why something is important to you.

Try this. Think of something you desire, a goal you truly want to achieve. Then ask yourself these questions and write down the answers.

- "What does this mean to me in the long run?"
- "What affect will this have on my life and on the lives of those I love?"
- "Why do I really want to achieve this?"
- "How will I feel once I've achieved this goal?"

Now that you've done this exercise, how do you feel about your desire or goal? Doesn't it feel more attainable now than it did before? That's because questions like these can help you figure out "your why." They give you a clear understanding of "why" achieving your goal is *necessary*. At that point, it's not just important; *it's something that has to happen*. Knowing *"your why"* creates the passion you need to find this level of commitment to your goals, and to yourself. Knowing *"your why"* carries you through the inevitable challenges that come while you grow and progress in life. It helps you turn obstacles into opportunities!

For example: What if someone's goal was to drop their bodyweight from 235lbs to 180lbs and "their why" was so they could look good in a swimsuit.

Do you think that's a powerful enough incentive to take the steps necessary to get down to 180lbs?

I don't think so.

But what if, despite a weak why, they were able to get down to 180lbs, do you think they'd keep the weight off?

I say no. More likely than not, they'd gain the weight back and in time would weigh more than when they started.

Why is that? One reason is that they had a weak "why". Another is because making a specific weight the focus of the goal causes loss of motivation once the goal is reached. Their subconscious mind says, "Hey! We made it! Now what?" And the "now what" becomes lost motivation.

But what if their goal was to be healthy and fit and their "why" was so they could live a fuller, healthier life and have more energy to do all the things they want?

Do you think that might work better?

It did for me.

Over six years ago I weighed 235lbs. Then I got fed up, changed my why and dropped 55lbs in six months. And, because my focus is being healthy and the benefits it gives me in life, I've kept the weight off ever since. And I look good in a swimsuit, even though that wasn't the intent of my goal.

But before that, I'd been on a weight yo-yo for years! It was only when I figured out "why" I really wanted to get fit, and changed my goal to focus on fitness instead of weight, that I became successful in creating the healthy body and lifestyle I wanted.

That's a subject for another book. And it will be. But I wanted to use it to show the importance of having a strong reason behind your goals. It's also a good example of why your goals should focus on a long term life benefit instead of a short term gain.

So start thinking of the reasons your new Blueprint is important to you. What does your new life look like, feel like, or sound like? What does your new life allow you to enjoy? Explore the possibilities. Try asking your subconscious to bring them into your awareness. Then, when the time comes to write them down, you already have them.

You Only Need to Know the Destination

Another thing to remember, once you've created your new Blueprint and are focusing on it every day, is that opportunities for growth and change will present themselves to you when the time is right. You must be able to recognize and willing to act on these opportunities when they come. Pay attention to the internal nudges you feel. These "promptings" and "inspirations" are how you'll get the directions for progress as you need them.

But we'll cover that in the next chapter...

Key Points
> ***Your new Blueprint*** is the master plan for your life.
> "***Knowing your why***" is critical to creating lasting change.
> ***Directions for progress*** will be revealed when the time is right.

Your New Blueprint

We all have things we'd like to change about ourselves. Even those who are honestly happy with themselves will usually admit to areas where they'd like to improve or grow. Besides, life is all about growth. If you're not growing you're moving backward. It's like your muscles. If you exercise regularly they grow and get stronger. But if you stop exercising they atrophy and shrink. You can't stand still in life because we aren't static beings.

But where do you start? How do you choose what to change about yourself? How do you decide what your new Blueprint will be?

The best way to start is to just *start*!

Now that may sound trite, but how many opportunities have you let pass by because you failed to act on them? I know that, for much of my life, I was a pro at watching opportunities sail past. Heck, sometimes they flew past so fast I didn't see them until they were gone. And the past results of my life are the perfect testament to my old inability to take decisive action.

Not anymore.

Now I act!

Why? Because past performance is not always indicative of future performance! Maybe we messed up in the past, but that doesn't mean we will mess up in the future! We can *choose to learn*! We can *choose to grow*! We can *choose to change*!

I did.

Sometimes I jump in with both feet now—because I know I'll figure out how to make it happen. And sometimes I gather as much info as I can before starting. But the key is this; I *do something*.

And so should you.

There is a Chinese art named Kaizen. Kaizen is about using the smallest possible step to create the largest possible change.

What if instead of exercising for thirty minutes a day you only had to exercise for five? Do you think you'd be more likely to follow an exercise routine that had such a small time investment? What about writing? Would it be easier to start if your goal was only one paragraph a day? What if it was a single sentence? A sentence a day might seem like a silly goal, but the point is this; it gets you behind the keyboard. It's the same with exercising five minutes a day. It gets you moving. The magic step is *to start*. Once you're doing something it's easy to build momentum. It always takes more energy to overcome inertia than it does to keep something moving or to speed it up once it's moving.

So *get moving!*

Start small. Just take a step, even if it's a tiny step. And then take another. Remember, forward motion builds momentum. And momentum creates miracles!

One small step you can take is this; ask yourself, "Where do I want to end up?" Or, "What do I want out of life?" You know that what you get out of life depends on what you put into it.

You might have the answer to these questions right away. And you might not. That's OK too.

If you aren't sure what you want out of life, this process can help. Ask yourself the question again. Only this time tell your mind exactly when you'll be back for the answer—a few hours, the next morning, be specific— then let it percolate, and move on to other things. It's important to set the specific time you expect the answer. This process engages your creative mechanism by allowing your subconscious mind to mull over the challenge. And setting a time for the answer prevents procrastination.

Often you'll notice the answer forming in your mind before the set time. When this happens grab some paper and write it down!

This process has been used by many great individuals to produce creative inspiration. It also works wonders to loosen the wheels of one's mind when it becomes mired with the flotsam that jams creativity.

Isaac Asimov, one of the 20th Century's most prolific authors, would tell his characters the end result he expected from them at night. Then he would go to sleep and find that part of the story written for him in his mind the next morning.

For many years I used this method without realizing why it worked. As a network engineer, I would joke with fellow employees and clients that, "I need to gather as much information as I can. Then I'll turn my brain loose on the problem for a few days and come back for the answer." And almost always, the final network design would come to me as if all of the pieces had been placed for me by someone who understood the intricacies of the project in greater detail than I.

Understanding the creative process of your mind will help you create your best Blueprint.

Change *Your Blueprint,* Change Your Life.

Designing your new Blueprint starts a process that changes your life. As you adopt the subconscious beliefs that make up your new Blueprint, you'll become aware of many opportunities to learn and grow. These learning and growth opportunities will help you make your new Blueprint reality. Part of this is the Law of Attraction bringing more of what you focus on into your life. And part of it is your new, heightened awareness. You'll see the world differently than you used to. Patterns might emerge where you saw none before. You'll learn to view others differently than you used to, perhaps with empathy instead of judgment. Maybe you'll realize when the perfect time to close a business deal has arrived. You won't know what these opportunities will be *until they arrive.* But as you act on them, you'll learn and grow into the person you want to be.

One reason creating a new Blueprint works so well is this; it moves away from the flawed method of behavior modification in which people attempt to change undesired traits with willpower. You cannot permanently change undesirable thoughts or behaviors through force or willpower. That method actually reinforces what you're trying to overcome.

Why?

Because forcibly trying to change a character trait—or control thought—puts an immense amount of focus on the thing you're trying to change. When you try to force a thought out of your mind, you are "thinking" about the very thing you want to stop thinking about, usually with powerful negative emotion. And when you try to change a character trait that you no longer want, you are "thinking", again with powerful negative emotion, about the trait you no longer want to have! This negative re-enforcement actually makes the thought or trait stronger.

Is that what you want?

Remember, when you focus on something, your Reticular Activating System (RAS) marks it as important, especially when it's tied to strong emotion. To put it another way; trying to force something from your mind or to stop a behavior by will power creates strong emotions. They are usually emotions like anger and frustration. But their intensity is strong. So that method not only marks the trait as important through focus, but it marks it as *highly important* through strong emotion. Then the RAS dutifully seeks out the thing you are trying to get rid of...and the cycle continues.

Trying to force thoughts from your mind or behaviors to change is a lot like sparring with an Aikido Master—your subconscious mind. The harder you push or attack the problem, the easier it is for the Aikido Master to sidestep and use your energy against you. You might get lucky and win a brief battle, but you'll lose the war. The only way to win in this situation is to choose not to fight, to go another direction entirely.

For example, if you want to banish the color red from your mind, the best way to do it is to choose to think of another color immediately when you notice you're thinking of red. If you realize you are thinking of red, instead of saying "I must force red from my mind!" Simply start immediately thinking of green. In time, every thought of red will automatically bring the color green into your mind. Then thoughts of red will defeat themselves without any mental warfare on your part.

Now who's the Aikido Master?

"A particular train of thought persisted in, be it good or bad, cannot fail to produce its results on the character and circumstances. A man cannot directly choose his circumstances, but he can choose his thoughts, and so indirectly, yet surely, shape his circumstances." (As a Man Thinketh, James Allen)

Creating your new Blueprint doesn't force anything to change. It *allows change to happen*. You'll use proven techniques to implant your new Blueprint into your subconscious mind. Then as your new Blueprint takes hold, your new beliefs will automatically start to overwrite your old, unwanted beliefs—think of it as tuning into a different radio station or changing the movie that you're watching. This creates a natural, stress free environment for growth and change. Then, as your new traits become an integral part of you, they will manifest in your life!

Now it's time to *decide who you want to be* and *become that person*. Open yourself up to the possibilities of life, to the magnificence within you. Unlock your true potential by changing what you believe in your heart.

It's time to take the next step in your personal evolution. It's time to Create Your New Blueprint!

Your New Blueprint
Step 1
The "Big Picture"

The first step in creating your new Blueprint is to figure out what your goals are. What life do you want to create?

Use the "Big Picture Worksheets" from Appendix B:

The seven pillars of *Your Blueprint* are listed on the worksheets:

- Character
- Communication
- Emotional
- Financial
- Mind
- Physical
- Spiritual

Spend a few minutes in each section writing down the things you desire most from life in that area. The idea is to brainstorm. So leave detail for later. Just get the ideas down of what you want most from life in that area. Come up with at least five things in each category. And *DREAM BIG!* Think of things that seem barely possible. Don't worry about how they will happen. The important thing is to get them down.

When you've finished the Big Picture Worksheets, set them aside and move to step two. We'll come back to the worksheets soon.

Step 2
Your Traits List

Your Traits list is the cornerstone of your new Blueprint. It contains the personal traits and characteristics that you need in order to create the life you want and achieve your goals. It's important that you identify as many of the traits you'll need to achieve your goals as you can. Detail gives *Your Blueprint* power. Identifying as many traits as you can now makes it easier to create a Blueprint that is a masterpiece.

Determine the traits you will need to achieve all the things you listed on your "Big Picture" worksheets. Ask yourself, "What traits do I need to reach these goals?" Think of people who are successful in those areas and model them. Study their actions, their traits and characteristics. Pay close attention to the traits that have helped them achieve their success.

I also recommend brainstorming about the type of person you'd like to be, independent of any specific goals. Do you want to be more loving? Do you want to have greater integrity? Do you want to be more outgoing? Do you want to be more generous? Do you want to be more forgiving? Think of things that will help your life be more rewarding even if they don't seem tied to a definite goal. Besides, you never know when an extra "positive character trait" might come in handy...

Use the "Traits List" worksheets from Appendix C. If you want to use your own journal or notebook, that's ok too. Just include the seven headings:

- Character
- Communication
- Emotional
- Financial
- Mind
- Physical
- Spiritual

List all of the traits that you need to reach your goals in each category. Also list the traits that you'd like to have—goal independent—to become the person you most want to be.

Here is an example. These are the traits I listed under my "Emotional" category:

Emotional: Abundant; loving; happy; peaceful; centered; rational; creative; open; fluid; patient; excited by discomfort because it means I'm growing and moving to a new level.

It's also important that you decide exactly what each of the traits you've written down means to you. Loyalty can mean any number of things to a person. What does it mean to you? Without clear understanding of the value associated with the trait, the meaning is up to situational interpretation. It's like looking through a dirty camera lens. You want to clearly define the trait so your subconscious, "knows what the Big Picture is".

Step 3
Write *Your Blueprint!*

Since your new Blueprint is a living document, the best method I've found for writing it is the "Desire Statement" format as presented by Michael J. Losier in his book "Law of Attraction".

The Desire Statement is designed to focus on what you are becoming and uses language deliberately designed to allow you to feel the positive emotions your goals will bring with no inadvertent backlash.

I prefer The "Desire Statement" format because it allows continual growth with no definite end date. After all, growing as a person is a life-long process and not something that should ever be "Finished". The Desire Statement also helps your mind recognize that these traits are continually developing. This reduces subconscious resistance, which makes it easier to attract things that help develop your new traits and characteristics. Finally, the point of your new Blueprint is to have a self contained document that helps you grow into the person you want to be and to develop the life you desire. Since some of the traits will develop faster than others, the Desire Statement helps ensure that slower developing traits aren't left behind or forgotten.

Let's walk through creating the Desire Statement that will become Your New Blueprint.

Title a blank sheet of paper "My Blueprint"; underneath that write "Traits that I desire". Then leave one line space and add this sentence, "I am in the process of attracting all that I need to do, know, or have to create my Ideal Blueprint." (This opening sentence follows the format found on page 63 of the "Law of Attraction Book" By Michael Losier. The sentence openings found on the next page also come from the LOA book.)

It will look like this:

My Blueprint
Traits That I Desire

I am in the process of attracting all that I need to do, know, or have to create my Ideal Blueprint.

That takes care of the heading and opening sentence. The next step is to take your traits list and write one paragraph or section for each of the seven pillars. Each paragraph or section should combine all of the traits you listed under the pillar. You might find that some of your traits carry over from one pillar to the next. That's OK. Do what feels best. Each paragraph in your new Blueprint should sing to your soul.

Use sentence openings similar to these:

- I love knowing that
- More and more
- I love how it feels when
- I love the idea of
- I love seeing myself as
- I've decided that
- I love the thought of

The idea is to make every sentence tell your subconscious mind what you want without creating negative feedback—when your mind says, "That's not true!" Using sentence openings like those listed above, addresses the *possibility* of these things happening and reinforces that you "like" or "love" the idea of being something. This method allows your subconscious to accept that you "are becoming" these things instead of balking because you aren't them now. And it does it without causing you to inadvertently focus on the fact that you aren't there yet. For the Law of Attraction—and our RAS—to do their parts effectively, *you must focus on what you are becoming.*

As an example, here is a paragraph from my personal Blueprint.

"I love how it feels when abundance is the predominate feeling I experience every day. I'm so excited that more & more I'm loving, happy, & peaceful. I love the idea of being excited by discomfort, it means I'm growing and moving to a new level. I love seeing myself as a centered, creative, & rational man. I love knowing that my Ideal Blueprint allows me to be open to positive change & growth. More and more I am fluid in my ability to share my emotions and ideas with others. I love the idea of being a patient, loving, kind, generous, and fun father to my children. More and more I'm a loving, generous, trustworthy, patient, and loyal husband to my beautiful wife."

Once you've written the body of *Your Blueprint,* close it with the following sentence:

"The Law of Attraction is unfolding and orchestrating all that needs to happen to create my Ideal Blueprint." (This closing sentence follows the format found on page 64 of the "Law of Attraction Book" By Michael Losier.)

Now you've taken all your desires and goals from your *Big Picture Worksheets* and on your *Traits List Worksheets* you've listed all of the characteristics and traits that you will need to achieve these desires. You've taken all of these characteristics and traits and created a paragraph or section for each in Your New Blueprint Desire Statement. That's great!

So, what's next?

The next step is to add what I call your deserving statement. The purpose of your deserving statement is simple. It's to remind you of all of the reasons why *you deserve* the things you're asking for in your new Blueprint.

I want to share how I came up with the concept of a deserving statement as part of *Your Blueprint*, and why it's so important.

I was listening to a daily "Fresh Start" call for the Personal Development Company and home based business that my wife and I belong to when the host, Kerrianne Cartmer-Edwards, told the following story.

> Kerrianne was talking with a good friend about her goals, and about the importance of knowing why she deserved the blessings the goals would bring, when her friend asked her, "Do you really know why you deserve these things?"
>
> Of course she knew! So she started to rattle off her answer, "I deserve them because I help others, because it helps my family, because I'm kind to people..."
>
> "I think you're missing the point." Her friend interjected and then continued with soft earnestness, "You deserve these things because *you're you.*"
>
> "You are a perfect manifestation of universal energy. You are a miracle. The very fact that you exist, means you deserve these things."
>
> When she said, "You deserve these things because you're you." It was a profound realization for me. I was so overcome with emotion and joy that I started sobbing. For the first time in my life I realized that maybe, just maybe *I really did deserve the blessings and abundance I desire!*
>
> That was when I created my deserving statement. And I use it with all of my major goals because it reminds me that, "Yes, *I do deserve these things.*" And it will remind you that, "Yes, *you do deserve these things!*"

Now the reason understanding that *you deserve these things* is vital for you to achieve your goals is this: When you understand this basic truth, it quiets the voices of personal doubt and opens you to the magnificence of your creation. When you quiet the voices of doubt, you open your heart to the voices of possibility and you remove feelings that may slow or even block your progress.

Let me say it one more time. *"You do deserve these things!"*

Got it?

Good!

Here are the deserving statements I use:

- I deserve my Ideal Blueprint because I'm me!
- I deserve my Ideal Blueprint because I'm a perfect creation of God!
- I deserve my Ideal Blueprint because I'm Infinite!
- I deserve my Ideal Blueprint because I'm a perfect manifestation of universal energy!
- I deserve my Ideal Blueprint because I use my abundance to help others!
- I deserve my Ideal Blueprint because it allows me to live up to my true potential!

I recommend using the first one in your deserving statement. If any of the others resonate with you, use them too. Or create your own. Either way, it's a good idea to know why *you really do deserve the traits described in your new Blueprint!*

Again, using an excerpt from my personal Blueprint as an example, your finished Blueprint should look something like this—but have a section for each of the seven pillars:

My Blueprint
Traits That I Desire

I am in the process of attracting all that I need to do, know, or have to create my Ideal Blueprint.

I love how it feels when abundance is the predominate feeling I experience every day. I'm so excited that more & more I'm loving, happy, & peaceful. I love the idea of being excited by discomfort, it means I'm growing and moving to a new level. I love seeing myself as a centered, creative, & rational man. I love knowing that my Ideal Blueprint allows me to be open to positive change & growth. More and more I am fluid in my ability to share my emotions and ideas with others. I love the idea of being a patient, loving, kind, generous, and fun father to my children. More and more I'm a loving, generous, trustworthy, patient, and loyal husband to my beautiful wife.

The Law of Attraction is unfolding and orchestrating all that needs to happen to create my Ideal Blueprint.

- **I deserve my Ideal Blueprint because I'm me!**
- **I deserve my Ideal Blueprint because I'm a perfect creation of God!**

OK. You've written *Your Blueprint*. Now what do you do with it?

I'm glad you asked because *that's the easy part!* Take your new Blueprint and yourself, go stand in front of a mirror and read your new Blueprint to yourself—out loud. Smile and read it with passion and enthusiasm. Make eye contact with yourself as much as you can while you read it. Imagine how you feel being the person you're describing. Feel the success, the joy, the gratitude, all of the feelings being this person will bring you.

I know you might feel silly doing this, but I promise you will be amazed at the profound difference this technique has over simply reading *Your Blueprint*. So go ahead and take the plunge!

Make a commitment to yourself *now* that you will read your new Blueprint this way every morning and *DO IT!* Make it a part of your morning ritual. What's it going to take, maybe a minute? I know that you can spare a minute every morning to *change your life!* And I mean every morning. Not for the next month or two, but for as long as it takes you to become the person your new Blueprint describes.

If your desires change down the road, that's ok too. When you find that *Your Blueprint* isn't aligned exactly with who you want to be, or when you achieve a certain trait and realize that you want something more for yourself, just revise *Your Blueprint*. *Your Blueprint* is a living document. It's designed to help you continually grow into the person you want to be. Throughout your life you should strive to be more than you are today. So leave mediocrity by the wayside and expect excellence from your life!

Next we'll cover the first thing you can do to maximize the results of Your New Blueprint...

Key Points
> ***Get moving!*** Forward motion builds momentum. And momentum creates miracles!
> ***Act on new opportunities*** as they arise and you'll grow into the person you want to be.
> ***Focus and strong emotion*** tell your RAS to mark things as Important.
>> o These are the things, desirable or not, that you'll notice and attract into your life.
> ***Attempting to stop*** undesirable behavior through willpower causes negative reinforcement and attracts more of what you "don't" want.
> ***Creating a new Blueprint*** allows change to happen by opening you up to the possibilities created by empowering beliefs.
> ***Read your new Blueprint*** to yourself in the mirror every morning.
>> o Smile, be enthusiastic, show yourself how excited you are that these things are coming to pass!
> ***Revise Your Blueprint*** when needed. Use it to continually grow!

Open Yourself to Learning and Change

Every adventure in life contains opportunities for learning and growth. Unlocking your true potential—which is what Your New Blueprint is all about—is one of the greatest adventures of all. Consequently it will present you with many chances to learn and grow. Now that you're accepting total accountability for your life, it's your responsibility to place yourself in a receptive state. Recognize learning opportunities when they arise and *act on them!* Otherwise they do you no good.

Keep that in mind. Now that you've designed, written, and are absorbing your new Blueprint, pathways will open in your life that were previously closed to you. This isn't because you weren't capable of these things before, it's because you weren't aware of them.

Think of it this way; you could stand in front of a blank wall in a house without knowing what was on the other side. As long as you don't know what's on the other side of the wall, you don't know what you're missing.

But what if you learned somehow that there was a breathtaking sunset happening on the other side of the wall? What would you do with this new knowledge?

Would you keep standing in front of the wall or would you *do something*?

It's just on the other side of the wall! And you really want to experience it!

But as long as you choose to stay in the house and look at the blank wall, you'll never see the beauty that's only inches away from you. And worst of all, if you stay in the house too long you'll miss every sunset!

The only way to see the sunset is to change something about your situation. You could leave the house. You could put in a window. You could take a sledgehammer and punch a hole in the wall. *But you must do something*!

Personal growth and learning are the same way. You must *willingly seek new opportunities.* When opportunities for learning and growth come along, you have to *recognize them and act on them.* This doesn't mean you have to be perfect at learning or that you have to learn with lightning swiftness. It just means *you must want to learn.* Being willing to absorb new knowledge allows you to see opportunities that were hidden from you even moments before. These opportunities arise as your subconscious mind, your RAS, and The Law of Attraction all work together to breathe life into your new Blueprint. When you act on these opportunities it reinforces their importance and helps you grow.

One Chinese saying states, "When the student is ready the teacher will appear." I also like to think that when the teacher is ready the students will appear. In either case, the act of being ready, of wanting to learn, acts as a powerful catalyst in your life.

I'll share an example of how this process manifested in my life.

When I started my journey of personal growth and development I had no idea what I was doing. I just knew there had to be a better way. That was all I knew; *there had to be a better way.* My marriage was collapsing. My children knew me as a brooding, withdrawn father who was so wrapped up in his own misery that he didn't have time for them. I was constantly depressed, bordering on suicidal. I felt like a fraud. I had no sense of self worth. I often said to myself that the company I worked for must be completely fooled to pay me the salary I was getting—It never occurred to me that I actually was (and am) an exceptionally skilled Network Engineer... It also had never occurred to me that I had any worth as a person. I felt like a waste of flesh, like I needed to constantly apologize to the universe, and everyone in it, for my existence.

Then came the day when my wife told me, "You'd better decide how important this marriage is to you. If you're willing to do whatever it takes to save it, then so am I. I'll stand by you." Then she left me to think about that for a while.

I didn't expect her to stay with me. But the knowledge that she might stand by me caused an epiphany. For the first time in years I felt hope. Maybe *I could do this.* Maybe *I could make things right.* When she came back I promised her that I would do everything in my power to heal the damage I'd done.

With the encouragement of my wife I began counseling. I learned the cognitive thinking process—as outlined on page 65. As I said before, it was as if sunlight touched my world for the first time in ages and my depression vanished almost overnight. Once I was solid in my application of that process I started learning about positive visualization as a tool to align myself with my desires and goals. That led to knowledge of Maxwell Maltz's Psycho-Cybernetics subliminal program—through Matt Furey. At that point I plateaued for a short time in my learning—because I wasn't ready for more.

Then a few months later my older brother introduced me to the book "The Jackrabbit Factor" By Leslie Householder, which opened up new levels of understanding for me and taught me how to write effective goals.

Next I discovered the personal development company, LifePath Unlimited. It was an easy decision. My wife and I joined LifePath Unlimited and became business owners and members of their global community. And I have to say being a part of a global community of like-minded entrepreneurs is a wonderfully uplifting experience. I'll let you in on a little secret too. My favorite part of belonging to the LifePath Unlimited global community is being able to listen to the Beyond Discovery calls that Patrick Combs hosts almost every Saturday. He interviews the best and brightest, people who are making a profound mark on the world and who embody the traits LifePath Unlimited teaches. It's like I have a back stage pass to the best interview series on the planet!**

Over the next six months I read many self help books by authors ranging from Denis Waitley to T. Harv Eker & Napoleon Hill. I discovered Anthony Robbins' *Get The Edge* home study course. Then I was able to take LifePath Unlimited's transformational home study course, *The Discovery Series*. And the process continues to this day. Every time I am ready to learn more, the perfect teacher or vehicle for that learning appears to me.

A list of books and courses I've studied—and recommend—can be found in Appendix C.

Again, I encourage you to open your eyes wide to the possibilities around you. Now that you've come this far you might as well take another step because:

"Man's mind, once stretched by a new idea, never regains its original dimensions." —Oliver Wendell Holmes.

Next we'll discuss some powerful tools that will help you on your chosen path?

**Vauna and I left LifePath Unlimited for personal reasons in 2011. My time with LPU was a huge growth experience for me. I'm now focusing most of my energy on helping others through my writing career.*

Key Points
> ***Seize the opportunities*** for learning and growth that life presents you, *and you will continue to receive more.*
> ***Act on the knowledge*** you receive.
> ***Trust*** that as you are ready for more knowledge and growth, your perfect teacher will be revealed.

Affirmations, Incantations, Declarations

Tools That Help You Grow.

The best thing you can to do achieve lasting success is to have a whole bag of tricks at your disposal. Does a magician go on stage with only one illusion?

Nope!

If a magician tried that, would they have lasting success?

Again, no!

You know there are times when one method will work better than another. And, though what you use and when is up to you, I want you to have a whole kit at your disposal. That way you'll always have something to help you on your path to lasting success!

I recommend using these tools in specific ways. But that doesn't mean you shouldn't get creative at times. Ultimately, only you know what's working. You need to be able to learn and adjust accordingly. Flexibility and attention to progress will take you miles farther down the road than blindly following someone.

Why?

Because when you pay attention to the progress you're making you can use failure as a learning experience, and *get back on track*.

When you drive your car do you travel in a perfectly straight line to your destination?

Of course not! Even if your destination is only a mile down a straight road, you unconsciously make thousands of tiny corrections to stay on course. When you first learned to drive you made large corrections and had to think about what you were doing constantly. But now that you've been doing it awhile, it's an unconscious action just like walking.

The same is true of your path to success. As you learn to be successful, you'll probably veer to the right and the left. That's OK! As long as you *Pay Attention* and focus on your target, you can get back on track when that happens. Then you'll be just fine. But if you aren't focusing on your target when you unexpectedly veer off course... I'm sure you know what will happen then.

So think of these tools as navigational aids. Use them to help guide you to your destination.

Affirmations

As you might already know, an affirmation is a positive statement you make about yourself to yourself. Affirmations are designed to help your subconscious believe something is true.

Traditionally affirmations are phrased like this, "I am a millionaire!" or "I have great communication skills!"

And they work, when repeated often enough with enough emotion affirmations *will* plant new beliefs in your subconscious mind. But there is a catch. When you tell yourself that you are something that you obviously aren't, a voice or feeling inside of you says, "But, that's not true."

This creates negative vibrations, which actually push away the thing you want. So while you're frantically repeating your affirmations, and your subconscious doesn't yet believe them, you aren't making real forward progress. You might even go into a backward slide.

Hmmmm. That's not what you want.

But you know that once you convince your subconscious mind—through repetition and emotion—that your affirmation is true, you'll start to see positive results from saying it.

So, how can you get the benefits of affirmations without any negative side effects?

By using a better method!

Michael Losier, in his book "The Law of Attraction," teaches how changing the opening line of affirmations from "I am..." to "I'm in the process of..." removes any negative backlash that comes from telling yourself something that isn't yet true. You can also start your affirmations with, "I'm becoming..." or "I'm learning to..." or other similar openings. Just make sure you don't use an affirmation that says, "I am..." unless you truly believe it.

I've listed a few sample Affirmations to get you started:

- I'm in the process of doing more than is expected of me!
- I'm learning to believe in and develop my capabilities!
- I'm in the process of seeing and feeling Abundance everywhere!
- I'm becoming a river of abundance!
- I'm in the process of becoming physically fit!
- I'm in the process of becoming healthier are more physically appealing!
- I'm becoming a millionaire!
- I'm becoming more successful every day!

- I'm in the process of becoming financially independent!

Writing your affirmations this way helps you achieve high levels of personal success faster than you'd have thought possible.

How fast?

I can't answer that for you. After all, each goal or desire needs a certain amount of time to grow into reality. But once you remove all the self-imposed speed bumps, I promise it will manifest in the shortest time possible.

As you know, your subconscious mind can be your biggest foe or greatest ally. It doesn't care if "what it believes" matches the facts. It just wants to make reality match what it believes. This fights you when *Your Blueprint* contains beliefs that go against your desires. But when *Your Blueprint* has beliefs that match your desires; it's like having a world-class coach in your corner!

That's why I encourage you to use the fastest techniques possible to implant your desires in your subconscious. It's critical to your lasting success!

Pay attention to that last bit.

Convincing your subconscious mind that *your goals are real and already exist* is the single most important key to lasting success.

Since using affirmations phrased with, "I'm in the process of..." is a powerful way to implant beliefs into your subconscious mind, I'm going to issue the following challenge.

Challenge:
I challenge you to write affirmations that compliment your new Blueprint!

Over the next thirty days read your affirmations to yourself every morning in the mirror. Be animated; show your passion and enthusiasm while you read them. Who cares if someone overhears you? Let them think you're a nut. Have fun with it. Do This and you'll find yourself quickly growing into the person you want to become!

Hint: you can use affirmations, and any of the methods discussed in this chapter, for all of your goals.

Then if you feel your mood slipping during the day, just repeat the affirmations to yourself and watch your mood improve.

Let's move onto Incantations...

Incantations
"Mini spells for your mind"

Technically an incantation is a verbal spell or charm used in a ritual of magic. But the way I learned them—from Anthony Robbins in his "Get The Edge" audio program—was that they are rhythmic phrases that reinforce your goals. They are designed to remind you of your goal, lift your mood (vibration), and reinforce your subconscious mindset. Incantations should also be easy to remember and roll right off your tongue.

Just like affirmations, incantations are said with emotion. But unlike affirmations, which are usually said once and in order as a list, incantations are repeated many times in a row. This repetition helps plant the ideas and goals of the incantation in your subconscious. And as you know, getting positive information—that matches and reinforces your goals—into your subconscious mind is the name of the game for creating lasting success!

Another difference between the two is that while I recommend saying your affirmations in the mirror, your incantations will work best when repeated while you're doing something that moves you toward the goal they match.

For example:

- If your goal is to get in great physical shape you might repeat these
  - "Every set and every rep makes me leaner and leaner!"
  - "Every time I hit the gym my body grows stronger and stronger!"
- If your goal is to become kinder and more compassionate you might say
  - "Every day in every way I grow kinder and kinder!"
- If your goal is to become financially independent you might say,
  - "Every day in every way I grow richer and richer!"

Another type of incantation directly commands your subconscious mind to do something to bring your goal into reality.

This is an example:

- "I now command my subconscious mind to do everything in its power to bring me the financial abundance that God wants me to have!"

In his CD course, "Get The Edge", Anthony Robbins tells how, before every speaking engagement, he commands his subconscious to help him reach out and help as many people as he can. And to do whatever is necessary to touch all of the people who need his help. He's done it for years. When he first started doing this, he would repeat it for five minutes or so. But the cool thing is that now his brain is so hardwired for the feelings and mindset that the incantation brings him, that he only needs to say it once or twice to achieve a total change in his state!

Both forms of Incantations work. Personally I switch between the two depending on what I'm doing. I've found that with activities that require more concentration, the short form works best. While the command form works great with activities that require less attention.

You'll have to find the incantations that work for you. Pay attention to how you feel when you say them. Do they lift your mood? Do they bring feelings of success and accomplishment? If so, they are great incantations!

Challenge:
I challenge you to create at least five incantations that are aligned with your new Blueprint! For the next thirty days make it point to repeat these to yourself at every opportunity during the day. When you Do This, you'll find that you can easily change your state and stay aligned with the path to your success.

Now you know about affirmations and incantations. Both of them are powerful ways to send information to your subconscious mind. Both are great ways to elevate your mood and personal vibration. That leaves declarations.

Declarations
A marriage between Affirmations and Incantations

In his book, "Secrets of the Millionaire Mind," T. Harv Eker says this about a declaration, "It's simply a positive statement that you make emphatically, out loud."

Declare is defined as, "to make known formally, officially, or explicitly (Merriam-Webster's)

When you make a declaration you're officially and forcefully telling yourself, God, and the Universe, that you are doing something or making something happen. This creates a strong emotional association to the object of the statement. And that highlights the goal or desire of the statement as something that is important to your RAS, which helps implant it into your subconscious mind. And that *is* the desired result after all.

Saying your declaration also raises your vibrations, which can synchronize it with the vibrations of your desired outcome. This draws your desire to you faster.

Why did I say declarations are a marriage between affirmations and incantations?

Affirmations, incantations, and declarations are all used to help your subconscious believe that you are becoming something. They are all used to raise your vibration as well. They differ in their phrasing and their approach.

Affirmations tend to be observations.

"I'm in the process of becoming a millionaire!" is a positive observation that you are growing into a millionaire.

An incantation can be an observation or a direct command—to your subconscious.

"Every day in every way I'm growing richer and richer!" is a positive observation that you are growing wealthier every day.

"I now command my subconscious mind to do everything necessary to bring massive financial wealth into my life while helping as many people as I can in the process!" is obviously a command to your subconscious mind to bring massive wealth into your life and to do it in a way that is beneficial to others.

A declaration tells that something is happening. You aren't observing and you aren't commanding. You're saying, "This is happening!" or "I'm going to make this happen!"

By declaring something you are combining the power of observation with the power of a command. Call it a commanding observation. Because, even though you aren't actually commanding your subconscious mind, the strong emotions when you make an emphatic declaration plants the information in your subconscious mind quickly.

Examples:

- "I release my disempowering emotional experiences from the past and choose a new, empowering emotional future!"
- "I choose to adopt new, healthier ways of eating!"

You aren't observing that these are happening. You aren't commanding yourself to make them happen. You are telling yourself, God, and the Universe that you are doing these things.

Declarations can be phrased any number of ways. Remember to keep them positive and focus on the desired result—as with affirmations, declarations are best repeated in the mirror at least once a day.

Challenge:
I challenge you to make a list of declarations for your goals! For the next thirty days read your declarations to yourself, in the mirror, every morning. Get excited! Be passionate! You'll be amazed at the difference this makes in your life!

As I said at the beginning of the chapter, I want you to have tools and choices that accelerate your success. There are times when each of these tools work better for you than others. You might decide that you like one type or you could *use a combination of the three.*

The key is to do something. Play with it. Have some fun and discover which format makes your spirit sing. Then use it!

Next we'll discover the true power of your emotions...

Key Points

> ***Start*** your affirmations with, "I'm in the process of..."
>   o   Read them to yourself in the mirror
> ***Incantations*** can observe or command, both work wonders
> ***Declarations*** tell yourself, God, and the universe that you are doing something
> ***Affirmations, Incantations, and Declarations*** are helpful when used by themselves, but when used along with Your New Blueprint, and Moving Your Feet, they have a magical Impact on your achievement of your goals and desires.

Harness the Power

Of Your Emotions

To Create The Life You Want.

Ah, emotions... They can send us into the clouds. They can tie us in knots. They can free us as easily as they can bind us. It all depends on whether we use them or react to them. Emotions are such a powerful driving force in our lives that if we let our emotions control us, we become a pin-ball bouncing from one situation to another in a quest to avoid pain and experience pleasure.

Sadly, when you live this way the pain avoidance techniques you develop almost always create more pain!

Here's an example from my life.

When I was a child, I had a Step-Father who, when beating me for something I did, would continue to hit me until I stopped crying. From this I learned that men don't cry and that crying meant greater pain. I turned this into men don't have emotions.

So, what did I do? I began stuffing all of my emotions away. Anytime I felt anxiety, pain, sadness, fear, any "negative" emotion, I would shove it in my emotional vault and slam the door.

Burying pain was my way of trying to experience pleasure.

But, as you can imagine, this created many difficulties. The act of disregarding my painful emotions actually numbed my "positive" emotions too. I reached a point where I hardly "felt" anything! Another problem with burying emotions is this; they have to come out sometime. I became an emotional time bomb. When my emotional pressure became too great, my "pressure valve" would open. Then I overreacted to everything!

I went on this way for years.

Then came the day, during my Junior year of High School, that Sam and I had a fight. Sam was one of my best friends. For years we did most everything together. But we had our differences too. Sam was mad that day because I'd flaked on our workout—in his defense it wasn't the first time I'd done this. And I was mad because I thought he wasn't treating me fairly and that a missed workout wasn't a big deal.

We were yelling at each other. Things escalated. All of the anger and pain that I'd bottled up for years boiled within me. I was so angry that I couldn't even think. Everything was rage. In a matter of moments, Sam became the personification of everything that had ever hurt me in my life. I pulled my arm back...and I hesitated. I heard a whisper of reason in the back of my mind, "Don't hit him. If you do, you'll never stop."

Without further thought, I slammed my arm into the plate glass window next to me. Because I'd also learned, long ago, that physical pain overpowered emotional pain and anger. It worked. My rage was gone in an instant. Only then, the severed artery in my wrist shot blood twelve feet across the room.

Thankfully I put enough pressure on the wound to stop my blood loss and Sam and my brother got me to the emergency room in time.

That event was an awakening. I realized then, that continuing on that path would certainly mean death for me. As I laid on the gurney with the ER Physician picking glass shards from my wrist, I decided that I wanted to learn how to handle my emotions.

Even so, I lacked self-belief and guidance and tended to only do what I had to...and it took most of my adult life for me to learn healthy ways to deal with emotions. In fact, it wasn't until I developed the subconscious belief that I could have healthy emotional patterns that I learned to control my emotions and use them productively.

For me this is real and lasting emotional success.

If you find yourself in an emotionally reactive pattern, have heart. It doesn't have to be that way. You can learn to develop healthy ways to harness your emotions, to make them work for you instead of against you. And, when *Your Blueprint* has healthy beliefs—about dealing with emotions, you can do it in a very short time too!

If *I can do it, you can do it!*

Trust me.

Yes, emotions can be unreliable and hard to control, but once you learn to use them properly you will find that you respond intelligently to situations instead of reacting to them. The ability to choose your response puts you in control. It also helps you choose what emotions serve you best in any situation. And that is a powerful tool in your quest for self-improvement.

"The faculty of the emotions...is the source of all enthusiasm, imagination, and creative vision, and it may be directed by self-discipline to the development of these essentials of individual achievement." (The Master-Key to Riches, pg 248, Napoleon Hill.)

Why are emotions important to your success?

- Emotions are necessary to harness creativity.
    - The ability to creatively approach things will help you learn more quickly. It also allows you to discover solutions and opportunities that might be lost if you only approach things with logic.
    - Creative Intuition comes through thoughts *and* emotions.
- Emotions allow you to be in tune with your spirit and your conscience.
    - Your conscience communicates with you through feelings.
    - Your spirit also directs and guides you with feelings.
- Emotions directly affect your vibrations and your vibrations attract or repel your desires.
    - Some emotions that lift your vibrations (and attract "positive" things into your life) are:
        - Happiness
        - Love
        - Gratitude
        - Abundance
        - Peace
    - Some emotions that lower your vibrations (and attract "negative" things into your life) are:
        - Anger
        - Hate
        - Ingratitude
        - Scarcity
        - Stress

You realize that emotions are also key to planting beliefs in your subconscious mind. But it doesn't matter if the emotions are positive or negative, it only matters that they are powerful. This means that when you feel strong anger, you're telling your subconscious mind that the object of your anger is important and to pay close attention to it.

Is that what you want, to attract more of whatever you got angry about into your life?

Well, have heart, because it also means that when you feel a powerful positive emotion like joy or love, your subconscious mind marks the object of that emotion as important too. And that *is* something you want! Because then you attract more of what you love or more of what brings you joy.

So, you have to ask yourself, "Which do I want more of in my life?"

"Do I want more of the things I feel upset about? Or, Do *I want more of the things I feel joyful and loving about?"*

That's what I thought.

This is why it's critical that you recognize emotions as tools that will help you on your path of success.

Remember, positive emotions create an atmosphere that encourages growth and success. Because of this, harnessing your emotions is important to maintaining an empowering, thriving atmosphere that nurtures your success.

Throughout this book, I've revealed many ways to create positive emotions and raise your vibrations.

Here is a quick review:

- Change your focus.
  - Find the positive in situations.
  - Focus on what you desire instead of what you "don't want".
- Discover your passion.
- Use the Cognitive Thinking Steps to take your mind off of Autopilot.
- Know "Your Why."
- Read your new Blueprint—and other goals—to yourself in the mirror.
- Read your affirmations, incantations, and declarations.
- Feed your subconscious positive and uplifting things.

Now, I'll reveal my secret method guaranteed to...

Supercharge your goals!

You know that emotions solidify your goals. They allow you to experience the feelings of success *Today* that achieving your goals will bring! Feeling that *success now* strengthens the power of your goals and that brings them ever closer to reality.

When you combine a clear vision of why your goal is necessary with the powerful positive emotions you will feel when you succeed. You're guaranteed to fast track your success. That's because powerful emotions *are the best way* to tell your RAS that something is important enough to shoot straight into your subconscious. And, as you know, your subconscious can't stand it when reality differs from what it believes is true. And once your goal is planted solidly in your subconscious; your subconscious mind works overtime to make it reality.

This is my recipe to "Supercharge Your Goals". First create powerful, positive emotions. Then, using these emotions, embed your goals deeply in your subconscious mind!

Here's how.

- Write your goal.
    - Leslie Householder calls this "Submitting your order to the Master Chef"
- Create affirmations that complement your goal.
    - Remember to use "I'm in the process of..." as their opening.
- Read your most important goals and affirmations every day.
    - Do this in the mirror and be animated. Because your subconscious believes you.

And finally...the secret ingredients that are guaranteed to ignite the emotional fire around your goals, *locking them in your subconscious mind!*

- Find images that truly inspire you.
    - Remember an image is worth a thousand words...
- Create Power Point slide shows that use these images as backgrounds and have your goals as the text.
- Do the same thing with your affirmations.
- Get a microphone and *Record Yourself* reading your goals and affirmations as "narration" with the slide shows.

- *Watch your personal power point presentations every day!*
    - o *Listen to your voice read your goals and affirmations to you while you view the words and inspiring images.*

When you *Do This*, you'll feel abundance, excitement, and gratitude engulf you! You'll feel that anything is possible! These incredible positive emotions will combine with your goals and affirmations to carry them deeply into your subconscious mind!

Because I believe so strongly in the awesome power of this technique, I personally created a power point template, *just for you!* As a bonus, you can go to:

http://www.YourNewBlueprint.com/bookbonuses and download the power point template (ppt) or (pptx). Then you can get started using this amazing technique right away.

How does it work?

Well, you've probably guessed there are a few things at work here. Inspirational pictures will invoke incredible emotional responses in you. Chose the right image and you'll instantly feel the emotion you want. Hearing your own voice read your goals and affirmations to you vastly multiplies the effectiveness of the message. Combining the emotions invoked through imagery with the power of your own voice is like using a laser to etch the message directly into your subconscious mind!

That's half the battle. Because as you know, your subconscious mind can't stand it when what it thinks is reality differs from what its sensory input tells it is reality. And once you have the goal planted firmly, your subconscious believes that it's true and fights like mad to make it reality. *This makes your subconscious mind the most powerful ally you can have in your quest for personal growth and success.*

Challenge:

I challenge you to download the ppt I created for you. Use it with your new Blueprint--and the accompanying affirmations. Then watch and listen to them Every Day! Do this for the next thirty days and you'll be amazed at the results you see in your life.

I encourage you to do this with all your major goals and affirmations.

I've done the hard part for you. I created the power point template. You can even use the images I included in it. All you need to do is use your words and voice to create the slide show and then *watch it.*

What's stopping you?

Next you'll discover the impact your body has on your emotions...

Key Points

> ➤ ***When you control*** your emotions and live in an emotionally responsive and proactive state, you are using emotions as tools to help you on your journey of success.
>   > ○ This will show you the way to true happiness and lasting success.
> ➤ ***Emotions directly affect*** your vibrations and your vibrations attract or repel your desires.
> ➤ ***You can supercharge*** your goals by creating powerful, positive emotions and combining them with inspirational imagery. Then use these to embed your goals solidly in your subconscious mind.

How Does Your Body

Affect

Your Emotional State?

Try something for me. I'm not sure how you're feeling at the moment. But I'm going to let you in on a secret that will improve it guaranteed!

Get up right now. Go stand in front of the mirror and smile as big as you can at yourself. A real Cheshire Cat Grin! Do this for one minute. Make it a smile that puts wrinkles around your eyes! Go ahead and do it!

I'll do it too and check back with you in a minute.

.
.
.
.
.
.
.
.
.
.
.
.
.
.
.

How do you feel now? I feel terrific!

It always amazes me how such a simple exercise can alter your mood that dramatically. And it's a powerful lesson in the impact our physical bodies have on our emotions.

The way you carry yourself not only shows how you're feeling, it impacts how you're feeling. Do you stand tall and look straight ahead if you're depressed?

No.

If you're feeling depressed and decide to stand straight and tall and look ahead with your head held high—all confident actions—do you still feel as depressed?

Right, you feel better.

So, what would happen to your mood if you stood in front of the mirror and scowled or pouted for a minute or more?

Yup! You'd start to feel emotions to back up that scowl!

So smile already!

Besides, it's physically easier to smile than to frown. And even being the fitness nut that I am, I'll let you off the hook for not working those muscles!

Let's do another exercise.

Remember a time when you felt confident and powerful, when you felt incredibly successful because you'd accomplished something phenomenal! Remember how good it felt. Remember what you were doing with your body.

What was your posture? How was your breathing? What was your facial expression?

These are the body language of success.

Now think of that time again. Remember it vividly, as if you were experiencing it right now. Put your body in the same posture as your memory. Match your breathing and feel the powerful emotions as if they are happening now! At the height of the emotional experience, make a tight fist and say, "Yes!" with power and confidence.

Do this seven times in a row, then repeat the process but change your posture. This time, stand or sit up straight and repeat the process seven more times. Repeat the process, with your new posture, seven times a day over the next three to four days.

This is called anchoring. When you do this, you're tying powerful emotion to a specific thing, in this case, a motion and word. By creating this success anchor, you'll soon be able to call on successful and powerful feelings anytime you need them!

The following diagram shows another format you can use to get the same result.

(This following diagram is based on the excerpt, "What Success Feels Like" from page 31 of the "Accelerated Learning Action Guide" by Brian Tracy and Colin Rose.)

Create a Successful Feeling!

Remember a time when it all came together, when you surprised yourself with your own ability

Pause!

Now create a vivid memory of your own success

Re-create what you were doing, what you were hearing, what you were seeing, what you were saying to yourself, what your body felt like, and most importantly re-create the emotions you were feeling

Sit up straight. Straighten your body. Pull your shoulders back. Look up and take a deep breath.

Clench your fist!

Intensify your memory of the original experience. Really FEEL IT!

At the peak of the experience say, "YES!"

Unclench your fist and open your eyes

Do this 7 times in a row. Repeat the process many times over the next few days. You now have an anchor that will ignite the successful feeling within anytime you need to call on it!

How does physical exertion affect your emotional state?

How do you feel after you've exercised?

How do you feel after you've done something physical, like gone for a hike, or walked to the store? You feel better than before you started, don't you?

It doesn't have to be something strenuous to affect your mood. It just needs to be motion!

Even if you're tired, you will feel better emotionally after you've done something physical.

Try this. Put the book down. Go do something physical for five minutes and come back. Walk up and down the stairs in your home. Do some pushups and crunches. Do some pull-ups or bodyweight squats. Walk around the block. I don't care what it is, just *do_something* and then *Come Right Back*.

I'll see you in five minutes.

Go on. I'm not typing anything else until you do this!

.
.
.
.
.
.
.
.
.
.
.
.
.
.
.
.
.
.
.
.
.
.
.

What did you do with your five minutes?

How do you feel now?

This is an interactive chapter and I'm doing everything I'm asking you to do. This is what I did with my five minutes.

1 set pull-ups
1 set dips
1 set bicycle crunches
1 set bodyweight squats
1 set pushups

And I feel invigorated and happier than I did when I started. I know you feel better now than you did a few minutes ago. Don't you?

This is because *your body is designed to move*. It was created to be used—responsibly. In fact, your body is one of the amazing things that actually works better and lasts longer when it's used regularly and fueled properly.

Think about it. The fastest way to make a body deteriorate is to sit completely still, do nothing, and eat garbage!

And as you realize, creating motion with your body has a positive effect on your mood. I don't care if you're in shape, out of shape, pear shaped, apple shaped, bean pole shaped, or athletically shaped, creating physical motion will positively impact your mood.

Physical motion is an amazing tool that will help you maintain the positive mental and emotional state you need to achieve high levels of success. And as a bonus, when you try something new physically, you stimulate new pathways in your brain which makes it easier to learn!

Start now! Introduce the habit of fitness into your life.

Challenge:
I Challenge you to start exercising. For the next thirty days take five minutes a day and do something physical above what you do now. You'll be amazed at the emotional boost this will give you!

There are also more subtle ways of using your body to affect your mood. As I mentioned before, smiling lifts your spirits. It doesn't matter if you smile in the mirror or if you simply make it a point to smile whenever you realize you aren't; *smiling makes you feel better*. And smiling lifts the spirits of those you interact with too.

Here's an example from my life:

I used to walk around with a grim set to my mouth all the time. Those close to me told me I always looked mad. I wasn't mad. I was depressed. But the impact it had on people who interacted with me was the same. My lack of smile was like wearing a giant "Leave me alone!" sign. And, whether I intended this message or not, it worked.

I was unapproachable.

Sometimes I felt sorry for myself that, "people didn't want to befriend me." But in reality I was sending out so many negative signals that I pushed away everyone that didn't have to deal with me.

My lack of friends was the direct result of the choices I was making and how I used my body and facial expressions to communicate my feelings to the world.

How things have changed! I almost always smile now. In fact, I can't think of a day in the past year that a smile hasn't been the predominate feature of my face.

Now people who know me say I'm one of the happiest and most optimistic people they've met.

I've even been told that "I'm annoyingly happy." This came from a person who was working hard to be depressed though. My guess is that this person became annoyed because my good mood was rubbing off on her—and interfering with her Blueprint about being sad.

Total strangers approach me all the time now and just "want to talk!" I've found that people are really quite friendly when you give them the chance to be.

And it all started with my choice to smile.

When you Smile, you open up the world.

Here are some other ways you can use your body to lift your mood.

- Stand or sit tall and lift your chin.
    o This posture fills you with confidence and communicates it to others.
- Breathe deeply and evenly.
    o Short, quick breaths are a sign of stress. Breathing deeply calms you.
    o It also oxygenates your brain and body.
- When you have to sit for a long time, take quick breaks every 30 minutes or so and move around.
    o Stretch your body and flex your muscles. This improves blood flow and re-invigorates you.
- If you find your mood slipping, take a minute and do something physical.
    o This changes your state and gives you an emotional boost.

All of these are ways you can use your body to control your emotions. Use them to keep yourself in a positive emotional state. As you know, staying in a positive emotional state will help attract the things you desire. When you're in a good mood you send out positive vibrations. And positive vibrations attract positive things into your life!

Next we'll cover the power of Music...

Key Points
> ***Smiling*** is a great antidepressant!
  o Smile every time you think about it.
  o Soon you'll smile naturally!
> ***Smiling*** is a great way to open doors of opportunity.
> ***Physical motion*** improves your emotional state and lifts your vibrations.
> ***The way you*** physically carry yourself directly affects your mood.
  o Carry yourself confidently and you'll automatically feel better.
> ***Create and use*** a Success Anchor to instantly recall feelings of power and success when you need them.
> ***Use your body wisely*** and it will serve you well!

Music Will Move You
Toward Your Goals!

Music moves us. It has a way of bypassing our conscious and speaking directly to our souls. Music can sooth us, influence us, and guide us. It affects us no matter our age or intelligence. Just look at a small child swaying in glee to music and you can see that it touches us all.

As you and I both know, it's this connection that makes music one of the best ways to affect your mood and change your vibration. You've certainly experienced this before. You listen to fast, aggressive music and you feel aggressive. You listen to mellow music and you feel relaxed. Sad songs can make you sad and upbeat songs can make you happy.

Once you realize the *profound effect* music has on your emotional state, you'll start choosing to use it to your advantage. When you notice a song is lowering your vibration, you'll change the song! When you notice a certain type of music excites and motivates you, you'll *choose to listen to more of that music.*

The things you hear, whether consciously or subconsciously, do affect your emotional state and your thoughts. If someone listens to a song with lyrics that promote fighting—even if they're doing something that has most of their attention—those lyrics get transmitted into their subconscious. And if they listen to that song many times... You got it! They're programming their subconscious mind that fighting is OK.

I've heard many people say that, they never "listen to the lyrics, only the music." Then they explain that it doesn't matter if the message in the song conflicts with their values because they aren't paying attention to it.

Really?

Beware; your subconscious mind is *always listening*. Why else does subliminal reprogramming work?

Choose the things you listen to wisely and they will help carry you toward your goals. Choose to fill your subconscious with messages that could easily conflict with your dreams and desires—by not *knowing* or *caring* what you're listening to—and you'll find you're fighting the current as you seek success.

Tip: Use motivational music to lift your vibrations throughout your day. Make it a habit and you'll be that much closer to the life you desire.

Motivational music is anything that lifts your spirits and creates the positive feelings that motivate you to succeed. It lifts your mood and your vibrations. And it's a wonderful way to control your "vibrational environment".

Anytime I can, I listen to music that motivates me. I encourage you to do the same. After all, empowering emotions encourage success. And anything that creates positive forward motion in your life will help you reach your goals!

Have you ever been around a person or group of people who were negative in their talk and actions? As you know, exposure to group negativity can quickly lower your vibrations and bring you closer to "their level". But what if you can't just leave? How do you keep their negativity from infecting you?

Music to the rescue!

In situations like this, I've found the best way to keep other's negative vibrations from rubbing off on me, or to "control my vibrational thermostat", is to put on headphones and listen to music of my choice. This creates my own personal negativity shield! And it works like a charm. I get to keep my positive thoughts and vibrations while all the negative messages bounce right off!

So load up your IPod or MP3 player with music that motivates you. Then carry your personal negativity shield everywhere you go. This simple action helps you keep your vibrations in line with your goals.

And *That* keeps you on track for success!

Now you know the power of music. Next we'll explore the power of subliminal messages...

Key Points
> ***Music*** is a powerful tool for influencing emotions.
> ***What you listen to*** impacts your subconscious beliefs.
> ***Listen to music*** that motivates you throughout the day.
  o This is a great way to keep your vibrations in tune with your goals.
> ***Motivational music*** lifts your vibrations and acts as a shield against negativity.

How Subliminal Messages

Modify and Reinforce *Your Blueprint*

Subliminal messages are messages hidden in something so our subconscious minds process them but our conscious minds don't. There are many different ways to deliver subliminal messages. Some examples are: words flashed repeatedly on a screen, drawings hidden within other drawings, even words embedded in music. Subliminal messages are powerful tools for delivering content to the subconscious, and they grow more effective with repetition. These repeated messages, delivered directly to the subconscious, help reform *Your Blueprint* by adding or reinforcing new beliefs.

When properly designed, empowering messages are used; subliminal messages create healthy, positive, and lasting change in your life.

My first experience with Subliminal reprogramming came through the use of the Maxwell Maltz, Psycho-Cybernetics Subliminal audio program. This was early in my path of personal development and I still had some very disempowering beliefs about myself and my value as a human being. I started using the CDs to improve self-confidence and develop a "Success Personality" and I noticed that I began to feel better about myself. However, I noticed the most dramatic difference when I listened—repeatedly—to the CD on achieving my goals and not procrastinating.

I'd been a champion procrastinator for so long, I couldn't remember being any other way. My motto was, "Why do it today if I can do it tomorrow? And why do it tomorrow if I can do it next week?"

Not exactly a formula conducive to success!

But then the most amazing thing happened. Within a few days of making the CD a part of my daily ritual—you listen to each one twice a day for a month; I started to *feel compelled to do things!* I found that I began to *take care of things NOW.* It was a strange and empowering place to be. I soon found that I could easily finish everything I needed to do, and still have plenty of time left for things I wanted to do.

I felt liberated. The new subconscious beliefs I adopted during that time have stayed with me. To this day I'm a "Do it Now!" person.

In fact, I still listen to my subliminal CD program every day. And I find that it not only relaxes me, it motivates me to continually strive for excellence.

As you've learned, subliminal reprogramming works. I highly recommend finding a subliminal audio series that compliments the beliefs you want in *Your Blueprint.* You don't have to buy it now. But if you do, you'll find it makes a tremendous difference in your life.

Which Subliminal Program Should You Use?

The subliminal program you choose is an important decision. If you are going to buy a subliminal CD program, look for these key points when deciding which program you will purchase.

- The exact messages used in the program are clearly outlined.
- The messages match your values and complement *Your Blueprint.*
- The music used is relaxing and enjoyable for you to listen to.
  - o If the music is enjoyable and in a relaxing genre that you like, you will be motivated to listen to it.
- The subliminal messages use a mix of male and female voices for each message.
  - o Male voices are more effective in planting the messages for men.
  - o Female voices are more effective for planting the messages for women.
- The purpose or theme of the subliminal messages is outlined with each CD or group of songs.

Follow these guidelines and the subliminal CD program you choose will have a profound, lasting, and positive effect on your life.

Next, we'll cover hindsight...

Key Points
> ***Subliminal messages*** are powerful tools for changing *Your Blueprint.*
> ***Subliminal messages*** help you reinforce the traits you desire.

Why Should You Look Forward?

Or

(The Rearview Mirror Effect.)

Now you're using your new Blueprint and moving forward. Your new story is unfolding and your life is changing before your eyes. They may not be big changes right now, but they are cumulative. Just imagine where you will be in a year! It's like making the base of a snowman; you start with a small ball of snow and roll it around. It grows and grows. And the bigger it gets, the faster it grows!

So have faith. As long as you *follow the steps I've outlined,* I promise you'll see dramatic changes in your life.

Here's a secret I chose to learn the hard way. But smile, because luckily for you, you can learn it, right now, the easy way. If you want to keep your momentum, if you want to build on it and keep wonderful changes rolling in, then pay close attention to this next sentence.

Look ahead, move forward through life!

People tend to look over their shoulder as they move through life. I call this "staring in the rearview mirror". But their life path, their story is unfurling in front of them. They can't move forward in life if they're staring in the rearview mirror!

If you find yourself staring in the rearview mirror, stop it. Take your eyes off that mirror and *focus on the road ahead of you.* If you do this one thing, your results will be extraordinary.

Imagine you're driving down the freeway at 75 miles an hour. You will *occasionally glance* in the mirror. That's natural and necessary. Sometimes you see something you must deal with and when you do, you deal with it quickly, don't you? Then you get your eyes back on the road in front of you, because if you keep staring in the mirror, you're going to get in an accident!

How quickly that accident happens depends a lot on how fast you're moving. If you're zipping along at 80 MPH and you stare in the mirror for even 30 seconds it could be deadly! If you are crawling along at 5 MPH, you might get away with looking in the mirror for a minute or a little more without too much damage—depending on what is going on around you.

As you've figured out, that means the faster you're accelerating toward your goals and desires, the more harmful staring in the rearview mirror will be to your success. And it means that the more you stare in the mirror, the slower you'll move forward in life. In fact, if you stare too long, you'll end up standing still.

Is that what you want?

Again, this doesn't mean that you shouldn't look back and take care of things. There are times in life when the only way to move forward is to deal with something that happened in the past. But the way you deal with it isn't by fixating on it, it's by taking care of it!

In fact there are many, many positive ways you can deal with things from your past that you're allowing to affect your life today.

I'll list a few:

- Forgive someone
- Change the meaning of what happened
- Become a student of personal development
- Find a good counselor
- Figure out what you learned from the situation
- Use it to help others
- Forgive yourself
- Make peace with someone

Only you will know which options are best for you. But the thing is to deal with it effectively *and get your eyes back on the road.*

Keep moving forward.

If you find that you're standing still in life, please understand that the very act of healing, of taking care of past things that hinder you, restores forward motion. It keeps you moving toward your goals. And it helps you create a healthy path for your future.

Face it, if you don't fix dysfunctional patterns from your past, you will repeat them. I know you don't want that.

The method that I recommend, regardless of the vehicle you choose, is this:

- Repeat these steps as needed until the problem is resolved.
    - Admit there is a problem.
    - Look at the problem only while you're working on it.
    - Learn from it.
    - Look ahead again and move forward through life.

A lot of people forget the last step. They keep staring at the problem. This either stops their forward motion in life or creates a huge accident.

I have a saying, "When you're swimming in the sea of memory, beware the riptides of regret!"

After all, people drown in riptides. And if they do survive the current, they end up far off course.

Denis Waitley—one of my favorite authors—has this to say on the subject.

"Each yesterday, and all of them together, are beyond your control. Literally all of the money in the world can't undo or redo a single act you performed. You cannot erase a single word you said; can't add an 'I love you', 'I'm sorry', or 'I forgive you'—not even a 'Thank you' you forgot to say."

To me this means that the past is the past and you cannot change it. It also means you should take care to live today as best you can, to prevent sorrow tomorrow.

Is there anything you could do differently, right now; to improve the way you're living? Start by asking yourself these questions:

- "Is there a rift I could mend in my life?"
- "Is there someone I might tell how much I appreciate them?"
- "Am I acting selfishly?"
- "Am I living with integrity?"
- "Is there someone I could help?"
- "What can I do to create a better world?"
- "Am I doing that?"

The best way to prevent regret is to live with integrity.
But just what is integrity?

Merriam-Webster's definition of integrity is this: *firm adherence to a code of especially moral or artistic values: INCORRUPTIBILITY.*

How does having integrity improve your life and help prevent regret?

In his book, "The Ten Seeds of Greatness." Denis Waitley talks about the Integrity Triangle.

The Integrity Triangle is a measuring stick you can use to determine whether your actions and words align with your values. It also helps prevent harm to others. Before you say or do anything you can check yourself by asking the questions that form the points of the Integrity Triangle:

1. Is it true?
2. Is this what I believe I should do?
3. Is what I say consistent with what I do?

I've created the diagram below to help you remember this key concept and to show how the questions work together.

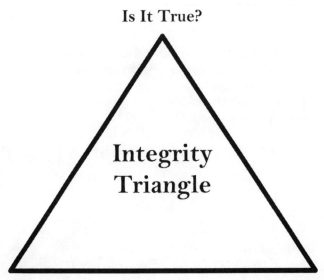

Is It True?

Integrity
Triangle

Is This What I
Believe I Should
Do?

Is What I Say
Consistent With
What I Do?

"Remember that it isn't enough to think the truth, act the truth, and speak the truth—though doing these in concert is to succeed in life. To be the most effective human beings, we must also consider the impact of our decisions on other people in our lives.

"When we honestly consider the well-being of others, before we decide to profit ourselves, we become truly rich in the deepest sense." (Denis Waitley, The Ten Seeds of Greatness.)

Living by these simple rules will help you move through life without having to constantly look over your shoulder. Living these rules means you know you're doing your best and that you aren't deliberately hurting anyone. After all, the most common causes of regret are wishing you'd done something differently or better, and wishing you'd not hurt someone.

As you can see, living by the three points of the "Integrity Triangle" will free you from most regret. It removes doubt about whether you did your best and it means you'd never deliberately hurt anyone. Another benefit of living with integrity is that it will help you inspire others to greater heights. Because:

"If what you are matches what you say, your life will speak forcefully indeed." (Denis Waitley—Empires of the mind)

If you don't feel that you have 100% integrity right now, have heart. Start applying the "Integrity Triangle" questions to your actions today. Use them to measure how your choices, actions, and words fit your values. Imagine how you'll feel once you make them a part of your life. Then the quote above will also apply to you.

What good is Hindsight?

Face it; hindsight is 20/20 because once something happens it's easy to pick it apart. It's over. Any immediate danger lurking in the situation is gone. So you feel safe examining all the, "I should have...", "I could have...", or "If only I'd..." scenarios without worrying about making the wrong choice. Do you know what using hindsight like that does for you?

It kills forward progress! And worse, by fixating on the problem you actually reinforce it.

Remember; *whatever you give your time, energy, and focus to you attract into your life.*

The reality is this. Whatever should haves, could haves, or if onlys, exist; you didn't do them. You dealt with the situation the way you did. But, "what if it was something out of my control?" you ask. Even then, you choose what meaning to give it. By doing that, you chose how it affected you.

You cannot go back and undo anything that you've done. You can apologize. You can do your best to correct things. Most of all, you can *Learn From It!* But you cannot change the past. So use your past experiences to help you have a better future. Use your new knowledge to make a difference in your life and in the life of others.

Simply put, use hindsight to learn what you can do differently in the future instead of using it to punish yourself for what you did wrong—or think you did wrong.

If you find yourself reviewing past experiences that didn't work out the way you wanted, ask yourself this, "What can I learn from this that will make me a better person?" Next ask yourself, "What can I do differently next time, with the new knowledge and experience I now have?" Then list the answers to these questions on a piece of paper. The act of writing them down will help plant these new insights in your mind. Finally, trust the answers you find and use that knowledge the next time you need it.

Then *let it go.*

This process will dramatically improve your ability to adapt. And that will help you stay on course during turbulent times.

Many great people have had terrible things happen to them but they still have gone on to inspire millions. What's the difference between them and someone who allowed their life to be destroyed by tragedy?

They took those things, chose their meaning, and used them to create the passion to make a difference in the world.

Take Oprah Winfrey's story for example:

Oprah was born into poverty to a single teenage mother in Mississippi. She lived through incredible hardships during her childhood and early teenage years.

But then, while in High school, Oprah landed a job in radio. She began co-anchoring the local evening news at nineteen. She did so well that she was eventually transferred to the daytime talk show arena. After taking a third rated local talk show to first place, she launched her own production company.

Today some of her accomplishments include:

- Academy award nominated actress
- TV producer
- Literary critic
- Magazine publisher
- Her, self titled, "award winning", talk show is the highest rated program of its kind in history.
- She has been ranked the richest African American of the twentieth century.
- The most philanthropic African American of all time.
- She was once the world's only black billionaire.
- According to some assessments she is considered the most influential woman in the world.

Her life is an incredible testament to the power of desire and purpose and the ability to find the positive in any situation.

Viktor Frankl endured the horrors of the Nazi Concentration Camps and discovered his ability to choose his reactions to these atrocities. He went on to write "Man's Search For Meaning", which has positively impacted countless lives.

There are also many people who came from "Normal" backgrounds and went on to have tremendous success.

The point is that when you choose to give something "bad" that happened to you a new, empowering meaning you're focusing on the good, or seeds of good, in the situation. This attracts more positive things into your life. It also means that you're choosing to use a "bad" situation as a tool to help you grow.

But you won't be able to do this if you're staring at the reflection in the rearview mirror!

You might not have a problem with this, but if you do...

Challenge:
I challenge you to stop dwelling on the past! When you find you're thinking of something in the past that you wish you could change, STOP! Ask, "What can I learn from this?" and, "How can this help me today?" Then write your answers down and with that information, continue to move forward in life.

When you live today, use the past as a classroom, and look to tomorrow, you'll find the road to success unfurling quickly before you. You'll even enjoy the trip!

Why Forgive?

Should you forgive or not?

That's a question only you can answer. I don't know your past. I don't know what you've been through. I imagine I have an idea where you're going—or you'd not be reading this book. I do know that at some point you've been hurt. We all have. And I know that true forgiveness is the path to real freedom. It is the only way to heal completely. And if you want to be truly successful, you should be whole, healed, and vibrant.

When you choose not to forgive or when your forgiveness has requirements, you're holding on to something that will fester and grow. And ultimately, the only person you're hurting is yourself.

Only you can know who the person you need to forgive is. Only you can decide if you should forgive them. They may know exactly what they did to you or they might not. What they did might have been done with hate and malice, it might have been accidental, even innocent, or it might have been somewhere in between. It doesn't matter. If you want to heal completely, you *must forgive them*.

If you don't want to forgive them, ask yourself this, "Do I want to heal or do I want to hate?"

Holding on to hurt, hatred, anger, or any other emotion that sticks inside you when you choose not to forgive is like keeping a dirty piece of shrapnel in your soul. Until you go to the doctor and have the shrapnel removed, it will continue to abscess and slowly leak its poison into your heart.

Is that really what you want?

In the Classic book "Psycho-Cybernetics" by Maxwell Maltz, he has this to say about forgiveness.

"Forgiveness, when it is real and genuine and complete, *and forgotten*—is the scalpel which can remove the puss from old emotional wounds, heal them, and eliminate scar tissue."

"Therapeutic forgiveness cuts out, eradicates, cancels, makes the wrong as if it had never been. Therapeutic forgiveness is like surgery."

As you now realize, only when the wrong has been forgiven and forgotten, as if it had never been, will the harm of your injury be released.

Challenge:
I challenge you to forgive someone! Think of someone who harmed you—or who you thought harmed you—and forgive them. Let it go completely regardless of what they did or what they've done since. Free yourself from the shackles imposed by your anger or pain and feel the healing begin.

*Just because you forgive someone doesn't mean you have to choose to be around them. Nor does it mean you are validating their behavior. It simply means that you are choosing to let go of the pain and hurt so that *you can heal and move on.**

Often the hardest person to forgive is yourself. But, ironically, you are usually the person whom you need to forgive the most. When you harbor anger, resentment, or regret toward yourself, you're focusing on something that you did "wrong" or something that you failed to do. And that drives a nail through the heart of your success.

Refusal to forgive yourself breeds regret and remorse. Mistakes you made in the past are in the past. View them as lessons to help you stay on course now and in the future. They should not be your focus in life. When you refuse to forgive yourself for past mistakes, real or imagined, you're keeping one eye fixed on the rearview mirror. When you have only one eye on the road, it's hard to see what's coming and it's hard to react appropriately to challenges that arise.

When you refuse to forgive yourself, you get stuck emotionally in the past. Holding on to hurtful feelings, and the situation that created them, actually takes a lot of effort. You might not think it does, but it's like digging and maintaining a moat in your mind. At first, you think you're just isolating the problem. But soon you find you have to keep going back to that part of your mind, to make sure nothing has built a bridge over your moat. And when you find a bridge, you have to tear it down.

The result is that you're constantly checking on the moat. It becomes a loose tooth in your mind. It becomes your focus.

Then when you start to explore similar things emotionally, or experience related situations, you get close to your moat. As you can imagine, spending a lot of time near your moat is a good way to fall in. It soon becomes a pattern for how you deal with these situations. Like it or not, all the focus placed on things you did wrong in the past firmly anchors them as the patterns you'll use to handle those situations in the future.

But when you learn from past mistakes and forgive yourself for them, you become a master navigator through the challenges of life. You develop the ability to react spontaneously and find opportunities where before you only saw obstacles. You develop the ability to try new things because you know that mistakes are just learning opportunities that help you stay on course. You learn that there is no failure. There is only learning and growth.

Then you are free to be truly successful. Because then you've learned the secret of using past failures as the building blocks of success!

Remember, to be truly successful in life, you must learn from where you've been and look to where you're going.

Challenge:
I challenge you to forgive yourself! Start today. Be gentle with yourself. Realize that mistakes are learning opportunities. They are the feedback you need to stay on course.

Next we'll cover life's ups and downs...

Key Points
> *To move forward* through life, keep your eyes on the road ahead of you.
> *Only Look in the rearview mirror when you need to*, to deal with a problem. Then get your eyes back on the road.
> *Live with integrity* and you'll minimize remorse and regret.
> *Learn from the past*, live for the future.
> *True healing*—and success—comes from complete forgiveness of others, and yourself.

The Ebb and Flow of Life

Life has rhythm. Expect this and you can use these cycles to your advantage. This knowledge will reassure you. If you are in a slump, something better is just around the corner. It means that a hard period is always followed by something easier. There is balance in everything, including your life.

If you think about it, I'm sure you'll recognize the pattern in your life. For most people it's a static rhythm cycle—where the peaks and valleys are always about the same. It looks like this.

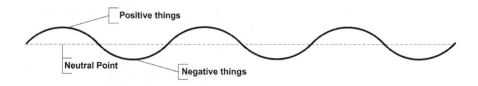

Does that mean when you're experiencing a peak in your life a valley has to follow?

Not necessarily. But, if you approach life with little passion for growth and change, as diagramed above, then, yes, it does. You'll go up...and you'll go down...and you'll go up...and you'll go down. There won't be any true growth. I've got great news for you though. You have the power to change this rhythm and use it to help you climb ever higher into the positive realm.

Imagine you're driving up a steep, winding mountain road. You climb for a while. Then the road levels out for a few miles before climbing again. The whole time you experience the rhythm of the road, *And You Climb Higher!*

Your life can be this way too. You will climb for awhile and then plateau—while you're growing used to your new level. Then, once you're ready to climb again, an opportunity to do so will appear before you.

I call that progressive rhythm. It looks like this.

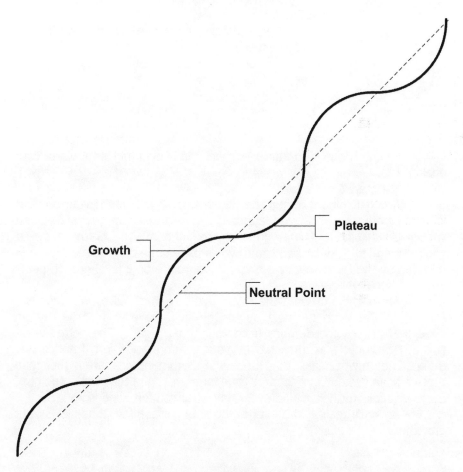

As you realize, the law of rhythm is still working in your life. You are still experiencing its flow and balance. Only now you're growing and experiencing greater things with each cycle.

It's easy to change your life's rhythm from a static cycle to a progressive cycle. Just follow these steps:

- Keep your focus on the positive aspects of each cycle as it comes.
- Expect growth and positive change.
- Express Gratitude.
    - When you plateau, be grateful for the new height you've reached.
    - While you're climbing, be grateful for the opportunity to grow.

*Hint: reading *Your Blueprint* every day will help you do these things naturally.

Follow these steps and you will climb ever higher toward your goals.

But there's more to it.

Another thing that impacts the rhythm of your life is your comfort zone. Sometimes, when you approach a new peak in your life, your subconscious mind will pull you back from the true tip of the cycle. If you're using life's rhythms to climb, you'll plateau before you're ready and miss out on the full extent of growth. But if you're on a level growth plane you'll go into a valley.

An example of what the rhythm pattern imposed by your comfort zone looks like is on the next page. The solid wave is the true rhythm cycle, without any interference from your comfort zone. The dotted wave is the rhythm cycle as impacted by your comfort zone. You'll notice two things. The growth peaks, that the law of rhythm intends, are higher than those reached when your comfort zone interferes. And the starting point of each cycle falls further behind every time your comfort zone kicks in.

As you'll realize, the interference of your comfort zone slows your growth.

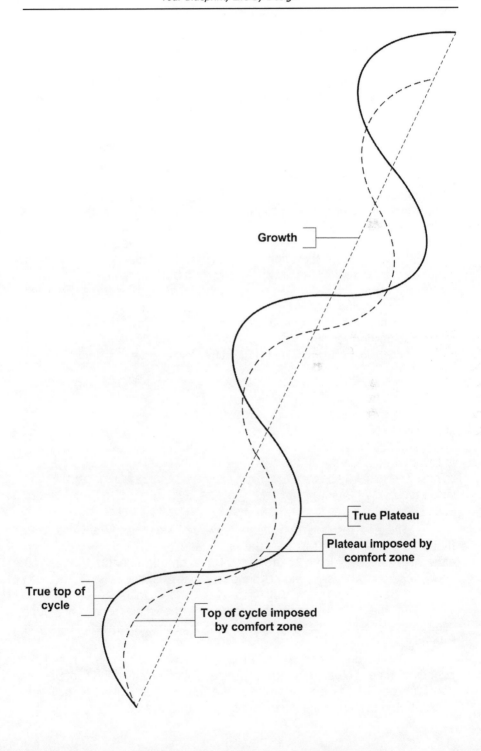

Why does this happen?
Because your subconscious mind is doing its job.

Your comfort zone is created by your internal beliefs and your attitudes about discomfort. It's also controlled by fear of change and fear of the unknown. When you stray too close to the edges of your comfort zone, your subconscious mind acts like a bungee cord and yanks you back. But as long as you aren't pushing the boundaries, it leaves you alone.

As a result, some people get trapped in the prison created by their comfort zone. It doesn't matter what area it's in; Character, Communication, Emotional, Financial, Mind, Physical, or Spiritual, they can't travel far from the confines imposed by the comfort zone's warden— their subconscious. In fact, even if they're trying to reach beyond their comfort zone; lasting success will be difficult until they learn to expand it, to make it flexible. If they don't do something to change their comfort zone; their subconscious mind will keep reeling them back in.

Obviously, this kills success. It locks people into patterns that keep them from growing and from being truly successful. As long as their subconscious mind is working against their desires, they will never experience lasting results.

When that happens, their life rhythm cycle looks like this.

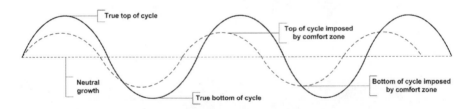

The end result is they don't grow, not significantly anyway. And though the valleys aren't as low, the peaks aren't as high as they could be either. Besides, the idea is to grow, not travel on a level path. And, as you know, a person who is growing experiences plateaus, not valleys.

Here's another way to visualize your comfort zone.

In the next diagram the center of the circle represents your comfort zone. This is the area where your subconscious mind allows you free reign.

The second circle is the area where you can stretch for short periods of time. The arrows represent your subconscious mind's influence. Your subconscious is uncomfortable here and actively works to pull you back into the comfort zone when you break into this area.

The third circle is the level of growth that is *Potentially Available* to you at this time. I stress potentially because as long as your comfort zone is confined to the center circle you won't realize this growth. You are capable of it! You have all the tools you need to reach it! But until you increase your comfort zone, you won't get there.

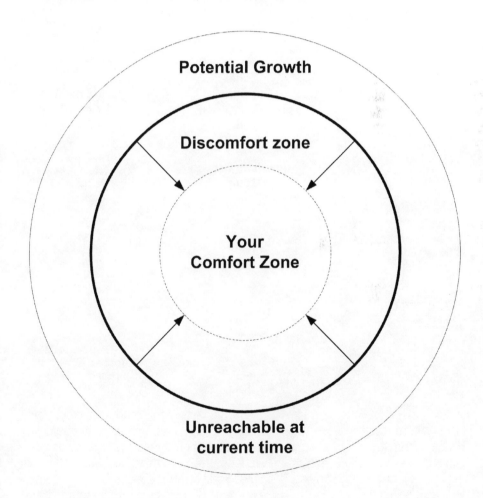

But what happens if you convince your subconscious that discomfort, brought on by learning and stretching to new levels, is a good thing? What does your comfort zone look like then? You still have areas where you aren't at ease, but if *Your Blueprint* tells your subconscious that this unease or discomfort is a desirable thing... Well, then it's a whole new story isn't it?

Now your comfort zone would look like this.

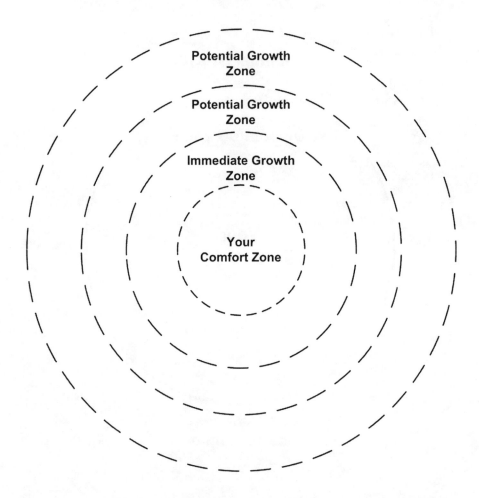

And then when you've expanded your comfort zone to include your old immediate growth zone, your comfort zone looks like this. Notice how your comfort zone has doubled!

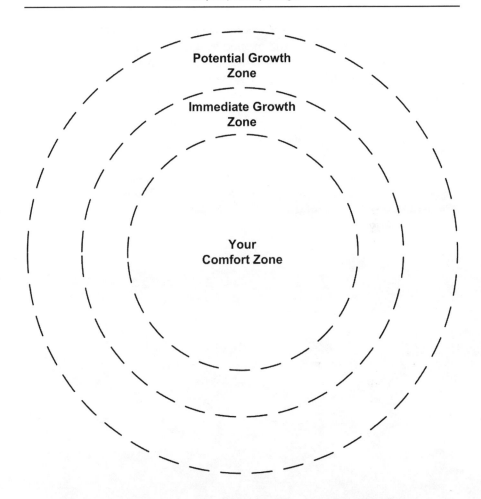

Now the next immediate and potential growth zones are open to you. And every time you expand to the next level of comfort, a new area of potential growth will open up to you. But as you've learned, this will only happen consistently when you re-program your subconscious to believe that the discomfort caused by personal growth is a desirable thing.

I want to stress that once *Your Blueprint* includes "the discomfort of growth" as a good thing, your subconscious mind will actually help you grow by seeking out ways to experience that discomfort! That means it will *actively* look for ways to help you grow.

What's the best way to include this new belief in *Your Blueprint?*

I recommend using a combination of affirmations, incantations, and declarations to plant this particular message in your subconscious.

A few examples are

- I'm in the process of being excited by discomfort; it means I'm growing and moving to a new level!
- I now command my subconscious mind to find pleasure in the discomfort created by expanding my comfort zone!
- I've decided that I always act in spite of discomfort!

I also recommend writing a goal, or including this message in your new Blueprint—if you didn't already. This will make it something you focus on regularly.

If you didn't include this in *Your Blueprint*, go to the goal setting workshop in the back of the book and create a goal about being excited by the discomfort of expanding your comfort zone.

Go ahead, I'll wait.

Great, you're back!

Now that you've written down your goal, make sure to open your awareness to opportunities for learning and growth. Be Courageous! Step into the realm of the unknown and stretch your mind.

Of course, stepping into your immediate growth zone can be more than a mental exercise. There are any number of things you can do to get used to enjoying this discomfort, which increases the size of your comfort zone. The real key is to make sure you learn something or do something new. That could be doing something you already enjoy, but in a new place. It could be introducing yourself to strangers. It might even be taking up a new activity, that you've always wanted to do but for some reason haven't.

The idea is to stretch yourself and stretch your mind.

Once you've created a dynamic, flexible comfort zone, you will reach the true peaks in your growth cycles. You will also grow faster because your subconscious mind won't cut your growth cycles short. When you learn to do this, you are free to emerge from your cocoon. It allows you to grow into the person you want to be.

Cathy Baker tells this story that demonstrates the power of stretching your comfort zone:

"One of the most powerful principles in helping my Mother do well has been to help her know *and* feel that she *can* do hard things!

"Her comfort zone has been shrinking for years, until now there is precious little she is able to do. Now it is beginning to expand, and she is thriving.

"Every time she says that something is hard (and with the very real combination of arthritis, fibromyalgia, and anxiety, everything really is hard) I say, 'It sure is, mom. It's a good thing you can do hard things!'

"The first time I said that, she looked at me like that was something she'd never imagined. But now she tries hard and is doing better than she has in years!"

Next we'll cover why you should occasionally reevaluate your goals.

Key Points
> ***Life has ups and downs***. The law of rhythm guarantees that a down turn will be followed by an upswing.
> ***Use the law of rhythm*** to create a growth plane and you'll climb to stellar heights of personal growth and success.
> ***Your comfort zone*** can hold you back. Create a flexible comfort zone and learn to be excited by discomfort and change. Then your subconscious mind will help you grow.

Why Should You Revisit *Your Blueprint?*

Perhaps you want to be a millionaire. You write clear goals. You create strong passion and find your purpose. You use the Law of Attraction by focusing on the abundance in your life. Soon, the money starts to flow into your life. But, something isn't quite right. Even though you're making more money than you ever made before, you're spending it as fast, or faster, than it's coming in! The result, you're still broke! Many "rich" people are only rich on paper. They make lots and lots of money, but they don't hold onto it.

Is that real riches?

Not in my reality.

It is possible to attract something into your life that you aren't yet ready to hold onto. This happens all the time. It's caused when pieces of *Your Blueprint* don't complement your major goals.

If the part of *Your old Blueprint* that deals with money reads, "I make enough to get by." or "Things always come up that I 'have' to spend money on." or "Rich people are evil." And you didn't address these beliefs in *Your* new *Blueprint,* then no matter how much money you make, you'll never hold onto it!

You know why too. When the reality of your beliefs conflicts with physical reality your subconscious steps in and figures out how to alter the physical world to meet its beliefs.

Personally, I want you to hold onto the things you attract into your life!

So, how do you change this?

You change it by examining all areas of your goals. When you wrote *Your Blueprint* you included the Character, Communication, Emotional, Financial, Mental, Physical, and Spiritual traits that you felt would help you become the person you want to be. These categories are designed to bring balance to your life.

What good is money without health?
What good is a strong mind without the ability to communicate?
What good is emotional health without someone to share it with?
What good is a life without strong character?
What good is spirituality without the rest of these combined?

Even so, the Seven Pillars of *Your Blueprint* don't inherently cover all of the possible things you might need to address to prevent conflicts in *Your Blueprint.* That's one reason why I believe *Your Blueprint* needs to be a living document. It must be able to grow and change as you do. After all, once you begin to grow in one area, you may discover a weakness in another that contradicts your growth. When this happens, just revise *Your Blueprint* to include an empowering belief in the previously weak area. Then the beliefs in *Your Blueprint* complement each other. And like harmonious notes, they strengthen the whole melody.

Take a moment right now and review *Your Blueprint.* Are there any gaps? Look for things that might need a little reinforcement or things that might be strengthened by a complementary belief.

Here are a few examples to get the wheels of your mind turning.

- Did you ask for Financial Abundance but forget to mention the ability to manage your money?
- Did you ask for a great life partner but not the ability to have a healthy relationship?
- Did you ask to write a great book but not to communicate clearly or to publish it?
- Did you ask to invent something wonderful but not to get paid for it?
- Did you ask for a thinner body but not a healthy one?

Look for areas like these and shore them up. You'll be glad you did.

Your Blueprint covers the grand scope of your life, but what about the smaller goals? We'll cover those next...

Key Points
> ➤ **Review** *Your Blueprint* often.
> ➤ **Look** for areas that can be strengthened by adding complementary beliefs.
> ➤ **Remember,** *Your Blueprint* is a living, breathing document. Reevaluate it often and change it as needed to keep you on course to your dreams and desires!

Goal Setting Workshop.

You know you are internalizing your new Blueprint when opportunities begin to appear that will help you achieve your ultimate desires. These opportunities might present themselves as ideas or insights. They might be opportunities to learn something. People might approach you about a joint venture. You never know how new opportunities will manifest in your life. And you don't need to know in advance what they will be. But you do need to recognize and act on opportunities when they appear.

That doesn't mean that you have to take every opportunity that comes along though. First, when presented with a new opportunity, you should decide whether it's something that will ultimately benefit you. Ask yourself, "Does this move me closer to my desires?" Some opportunities might change your course slightly. Some might alter the path dramatically but keep the same destination. Some might open up a path you'd never imagined was possible. Think of these opportunities as signposts. Each one will give you information that can help you reach your ultimate desire. Only you can decide which to pursue. But once you've decided an opportunity is a path you want to take, you must *Take Massive Action!* Dive in headfirst.

"Leap and the net will appear." – Zen Saying

Remember, you don't need to know the path; you just need to know your destination and be able to get to the next signpost. The path will present itself to you along the way.

When you drive through a winding mountain pass, you might only see a few hundred feet of road before you at a time. Yet you are able to safely navigate by paying attention to the road as you round each bend. You know where you are going and you know the road is there; that is enough to give you the faith necessary to start your journey. You don't need to know all the details of the trip before you leave.

In fact, when speaking of goals, feeling that you have to know all of the details of the trip before you start is a great way to guarantee you'll never leave.

Once you've made the decision to pursue an opportunity, write it down in goal form. Until you do this it's not really a decision.

Writing down your goal is imperative for many reasons:

- A written goal means you've committed yourself to that destination.
- A written goal solidifies your intent.
- A written goal allows you to create a detailed image of your destination.
- A written goal tells your RAS and thereby your subconscious that you are serious.
- A written goal is something you can read every day to heighten your excitement about the journey you are taking.

Yet around 90% of the people who want something are unwilling to *write it down*. They come up with excuses about time and effort or how writing it down is silly because they already know what they want.

Really?

If a person is unwilling to take this first, critical step toward achieving their goals, do they really know what they want? Do they have the desire they need to follow through?

When talking about reading declarations to yourself in the mirror— something that some people might find as silly as writing down their goals, T. Harv Eker says this:

"I'd rather be really hokey and really rich than really cool and really broke." — T. Harv Eker, Secrets of the Millionaire Mind

I think it couldn't be said better.

Are you one of the 10% who is willing to write down your goals?

If you've read this far I'm betting you are. And that's great!

If you're not, then it's time to ask yourself, "how serious am I?"

Well, *just how serious are you?*

Think about it...

Goal Formats

There are two types of goal formats that I recommend. One is the Desire statement—as I outlined in the chapter on creating your new Blueprint. The other format is a gratitude statement.

Gratitude Statements

I learned about gratitude statements in Leslie Householder's book, "The Jackrabbit Factor". A gratitude statement is a goal written in present tense, focusing on the gratitude you feel now that you have achieved your goal. It also focuses on the positive feelings and the positive results that achieving your goal has brought you. A gratitude statement has a future date on the top of the page. This is the target date of the goal.

The date at the top of your gratitude statement is important because *this is the date by which you believe you can achieve your goal.* The date needs to be far enough away to be realistic, yet close enough to inspire you to really move and to keep you excited about your goal. Another thing the date does is allow your subconscious mind to believe in this outcome. Reading the future date at the top of your gratitude statement before you read the body, tells your subconscious that "by this date the following things are true". You're then free to experience all of the feelings of achievement and gratitude that accompany the realization of your goal without any subconscious backlash.

This is similar to the reason affirmations opened with, "I'm in the process of..." work better than those that simply say, "I am..."

It's important that your gratitude statement focuses on your goal in a positive sense. For example; if your goal is about being financially free (rid of debt), you might use statements like this, "I'm so grateful now that I am financially free and can easily pay for anything I want or need." That situation will come to pass when you've either paid off all of the debt you currently have or when you make so much money that it's not a concern—in which case I hope you have met all of the obligations you have to debtors.

The point is that using language, which places emphasis on the positive outcome of your goal, uses the Law of Attraction to draw it into your life. While statements like, "I'm grateful now that I've paid off all my debt." unintentionally places focus on "debt" which attracts more of that.

I know that's not what you want!

Your gratitude statement needs to be written in positive tense—as if you'd already achieved your goal, because otherwise the statements can backfire.

If your goal is to drop 50 lbs in five months and you use statements like, "I'm so glad that in five months I'll have reduced my weight by 50lbs!" What you're actually telling your subconscious is this, "five months from now I'll have 50 extra pounds that I need to drop to meet my ideal weight." Obviously that's not what you want! But the statement, "I'm so grateful now that I'm lean and muscular and weigh 180lbs." tells your subconscious mind that by the date of this goal, you weigh 180lbs and are lean and muscular.

Which do you think serves your purpose better?

*Note: If you're wondering why I never use the word "Lose" in relation to bodyweight, just ask yourself, "what do I do when I lose something?" Right! Well, your subconscious works the same way. It wants to find things that are "lost". When you reach your ideal weight or body shape, the last thing you want is for your subconscious mind to start "looking for" the weight you "lost".

When creating gratitude statements it's important to use as much detail as possible. Think of all of the positive things that will happen once your goal is reached and use them in your gratitude statement. It's important to think of the rewards of achieving your goal and the feelings these rewards will bring you.

To help in this process, ask yourself the following questions:

- How will I feel when I accomplish my goal?
- What will my life be like when I achieve my goal?
  - How will this feel?
- What will the positive changes in my life be?
  - How will this feel?
- What effect will it have on those I love?
  - How will I feel about this?
- What specific differences will it make in my life?
  - How will I feel about these differences?
- What material, physical, financial, spiritual, etc. things will I now enjoy because I've successfully met my goal?
  - How will I feel about all of these?

Use the answers to these questions to create the detailed body of your gratitude statement. The questions about your feelings give you the context of the reward. Meaning: If you have a new car (reward) and you feel excited and grateful for it, then a sentence in your gratitude statement might be; "I'm so excited and grateful now that I have a bright red Porsche!"

More detail is always better because it makes it easier to really *visualize* your success and *feel* the emotions your success and accomplishment brings. When you have enough detail that reading your gratitude statement fills you with incredible positive emotions, you're on the right track.

When I read my gratitude statements, I feel like my body is tingling with positive energy. The same is true when I read my desire statements. It might be different for you, but if you pay attention to the feelings you have when you read your gratitude statement, *you'll know when you have it right.*

Here is an example of a gratitude statement. This is one of the first gratitude statements I ever wrote. I used this to get the perfect motorcycle for the budget I had to work with at the time.

Sept 10 2008

I am so grateful for the stylish and comfortable motorcycle I own. I am happy that the Lord helped me find a motorcycle that is reliable, fast, and good looking for $2000.00. It is so fun to ride my motorcycle. I love the way it corners and accelerates and I love the freedom I feel when I ride. I am very fond of the fat rear tire and the way it grips the road. I am so grateful that the Lord helped me find my motorcycle and that I still have money to meet my financial obligations! I am having fun sharing the wonderful methods I learned and used to meet this goal.

Okay, so it's not Emerson, But It Worked!

I had the money. I had the desire. I was having trouble finding the motorcycle I wanted at the price I was willing to pay. So I wrote this gratitude statement and I dated it four days from the time I wrote it. Then *I set aside all disbelief* and kept looking for that perfect bike.

One day later, I found the bike I wanted listed on Craig's list. It was $3000.00 though. So I kept looking. But mentally I kept going back to the $3000.00 bike. I just knew it was the bike I wanted...but the price wasn't right.

The next morning my wife was helping me look and she came across a bike on Ebay that she thought I'd be interested in. It had one bid on it for $1500.00 and the reserve hadn't been met. There were four hours left in the auction.

I looked at the web page, and It Was *The Same Bike I Wanted!* The seller was auctioning it on Ebay at the same time they were listing it on Craig's List.

So I placed my bid at $2000.00... That was the reserve amount and *I Won The Auction!*

This was two days before the date I'd written on the top of my gratitude statement. I wanted to pick up the bike on the third day, but the seller needed to do something to it first and I ended up taking possession of my new ride on the exact date I'd written on the top of my gratitude statement.

Coincidence?

You tell me.

Desire Statement or Gratitude Statement
Which should you use?

Desire statements work best with large, multi-faceted goals or things that, by nature, should continually evolve. That's why I recommend using a desire statement to write *Your Blueprint*. A desire statement can be continuously relevant to your changing life while a gratitude statement might unintentionally create a "stopping point" for your growth.

Gratitude statements work best when you have a definite date by which you want to accomplish something and you know exactly what it is you want to achieve. I recommend using gratitude statements as the bricks with which to build the life you've designed in your new Blueprint. Call them sub-goals and your new Blueprint your major goal.

I break it down this way:

- Blueprint

    o   Gratitude Statement

        ▪   Plan of action

            •   Monthly steps

                o   Weekly steps

                    ▪   Daily steps

This diagram on the following page demonstrates a high-level view of the process.

Blueprint (Desire Statement)

Gratitude Statement	Gratitude Statement	Gratitude Statement	Gratitude Statement
Plan of Action	Plan of Action	Plan of Action	Plan of Action
Monthly Steps	Monthly Steps	Monthly Steps	Monthly Steps
Weekly Steps	Weekly Steps	Weekly Steps	Weekly Steps
Daily Steps	Daily Steps	Daily Steps	Daily Steps

Your Blueprint isn't the only desire statement you'll write. In fact, because finances are such an important part of a successful life, I also recommend having a desire statement that specifically covers your financial future. Each desire statement you create will have the potential for many sub-goals in it. Use gratitude statements to write your sub-goals—Think of them as the building blocks of the master goal outlined in your desire statement. Then create your plan—do the best you can here. Your plan might be: "I'm going to find a mentor who will help me learn this task." Then break your plan down into logical steps. Your Monthly steps are formed by your Weekly steps which are formed by your Daily steps. No matter what, always take daily steps! Oh, something like; "I will read my Blueprint every day..." and "I will perform one income producing activity every day" are good examples of daily steps to take.

Create Your Goals!

Now you have a clear understanding of the differences between desire statements and gratitude statements, as well as when to use them.

Over the next few pages you'll discover the topics you'll use for your gratitude statements—I'm going to call them "goals" for the rest of the chapter.

There is a reason we're doing an exercise similar the "Big Picture Worksheets" now. You've created Your New Blueprint and you've been reading it every morning. You've even downloaded the Power Point Template, put *Your Blueprint* in it, and recorded your voice reading you *Your Blueprint*. These exercises have undoubtedly opened your mind to new possibilities, things you didn't know you could even dream about before. I know you don't want to miss out on any new goal that might be on your radar now.

So, the first part of the process is brainstorming about the things you want most in life. Each of the following sheets is labeled with one of the Pillars of *Your Blueprint*. Use these pages and take two minutes per page to write down all of the things you can think of that you'd like to see, do, have, experience, or learn in each of the categories.

Think of things that are fantastic!

Think of things that are barely believable!

Really stretch yourself. Be spontaneous and keep your pen moving the whole time. Trust what your gut is telling you. You want to come up with things that inspire you to take massive action, like you've never taken it before! Just because you don't know how you'll do it doesn't mean you can't do it! If you can think of it, and it doesn't defy the laws of nature, *YOU CAN ACHIEVE IT!*

Heck, with the way science is advancing, even something that appears to defy the laws of nature might be possible for you...

Start now! I'll wait.

Character

Communication

Emotional

Financial

Mind

Physical

Spiritual

Now that you have an impressive list of things you want to accomplish or experience, follow these steps.

1. Go back through your lists. What is the time frame for each goal you wrote down. When do you want to achieve it? Is it something that would be nice to do in the next twenty years, or is it something you want to do within the next year or even the next six months? Mark a number representing how many years you have to accomplish it next to each item.
    a. This gives you a good idea of the date to write at the top of the goal.
    b. These dates need to be close enough to keep you excited, but just far enough away to be realistic.
2. Go through the lists and select the "top five" from each Blueprint Pillar.
    a. Determine if any of the closer goals are logical steps toward your longer term goals. You can combine these if they are.
3. Write a gratitude statement for the number 1 item from each Blueprint pillar.
    a. You'll review this every day along with *Your Blueprint*.
4. For the other four in each category, you can either write a gratitude statement that includes them all or individual gratitude statements.
    a. These you'll review at least once a week.
5. Come up with a plan for achieving each goal.
6. Set aside the rest of the things you listed for now. You can come back to them later when you've accomplished some of your more important goals.

It's time to breathe life into these goals. For each of the goals you wrote in step 3, do something *Today*, even *Right Now* that sets it in motion.

Challenge:
*   ***Do something right now that moves you toward the realization of each goal you wrote.***
*   ***Review your new gratitude statements every day.***
*   ***Take one action step every day toward each goal.***

Now you have a new Blueprint and sub-goals. Is there anything else that will help guarantee your success?

Key Points

> *Sub-goals* are the building blocks of *Your Blueprint*. They are the smaller steps that will carry you on the road to success.

> *Write a separate goal* for the top desire from each pillar of *Your Blueprint*.

  o Review this every day.

> *Do something* every day that carries you toward your goals.

> *Immediately* take action when you create a goal.

Persistence

The Magic Ingredient for Your Success

Are you willing to carry on until you achieve your goal?

Are you willing to carry on, *no matter what opposition you encounter?*

If you answered yes, then you understand the level of persistence necessary to achieve true success. Persistence is critical when creating the drive you need to turn obstacles into opportunities. Every time you fail at something your mind and body will remember the successful parts of the attempt—as long as that is what you focus on. When these successful memories are combined with persistence you're giving your mind and body more data to work with; you're giving yourself more information to learn to do it right!

When learning to walk, infants don't give up because it's difficult. They persevere! No one told them giving up was an option. So they take all the bumps and knocks that happen while they learn to walk and they shake them off. Then they get back up and try again!

Guess what?

We were all infants once... We can recapture that type of perseverance!

Humans are creatures full of curiosity. We're born with drive to discover how to do things, to succeed. And we do. As young children we discover and learn and grow at an amazing rate. It's not until we're older that we learn how to take the easy way out.

Failure—quitting—is not a concept small children understand. It is something that is learned and modeled. Luckily that means it can be unlearned too.

Learn to have the persistence of a small child!

Many people come close to achieving their goals, only to give up in the last stretch! They put in time and effort. But then something happens, and they give up or lose their passion and slip off the path that would carry them to their dream, when, if they'd only persisted a little longer, they'd have crossed their finish line.

Then there are the people who throw in their towel at the first sign of real struggle. They jump off the path to success before they even have a chance to grow.

Well, I've got news for you. Learning to be truly successful, creating your new Blueprint and becoming the person you want to be is a path that's going to have struggles on it!

Anything in life worth having takes effort!

So take these obstacles and reframe them. Give them different meanings by changing your focus.

Instead of, "Oh my gosh! I crashed my motorcycle!" it becomes, "What a tremendous learning opportunity! I'm glad I'm alright; and now I know how to handle that corner next time."

Instead of, "Oh No! My investments are tanking because the stock market is going down!" it becomes, "This is great! Now I can buy even more stocks! And when the market recovers I'll be even farther ahead!"

Remember; all of the challenges you face on your path to achieving your goals are opportunities for learning and growth.

Thomas Edison discovered 10,000 ways, "not to make a light bulb" before he discovered the way that worked.

Why?

Because he persevered!

Michael Jordan tried out for the Varsity Basketball team in 10th grade and was rejected because at 5ft 11in tall, he was deemed too short. But he didn't give up on his dream. Instead he joined the Junior Varsity Squad and became the star player with several 40 point games!

Over the next summer he practiced rigorously. And he grew 4 inches! As a junior, he earned a spot on the Varsity Team. Over the next two years he averaged 20 points a game.

His stellar High school career landed him a scholarship at North Carolina. He played there for three years before participating in the 1984 NBA draft.

Michael Jordan not only went on to become the most celebrated player in NBA history, but he went back to North Carolina and finished his college degree three years into his NBA career.

To his credit, Michael Jordan has 25 last second, game winning shots. 24 of those shots were during the last 10 seconds, 8 were at the buzzer, and one was in the last 12 seconds of the game.

www.NBA.com says, "By acclimation Michael Jordan is the greatest basketball player of all time."

"The difference between a great athlete and a mediocre athlete lies not only in their skill, but in their desire to succeed." — Unknown

What do Thomas Edison and Michael Jordan have in common? Both of them *knew how to persevere.* It is this trait that made them both champions.

What about you?

When you choose to give up on your goals or desires, you're giving up on yourself. You're making the decision to not take the shots that could win the game for you. Sure, you might miss and lose the game anyway. But losing a game isn't losing the season. And when you decide not to take the shot...

"You miss 100% of the shots you don't take." — Wayne Gretski

Take The Shot!

Otherwise you're saying that your fear of failure or your fear of struggle is more important than your purpose in life.

When I feel doubt about the path I'm on, I ask myself these questions:

- "Who am I to hoard the gifts I've been given?"
- "Who am I cheating if I fail to act?"
- "What good will remain undone if I selfishly choose to give up at the last hour?"

When you feel like quitting, when things have gotten a little tough and you consider stopping before you've realized your dreams, ask yourself the questions above.

Make a decision today to put in the effort. Side step, step over, even plow through the obstacles that rise before you. Is it a mountain or a mole-hill? Your perception makes all the difference.

Make the decision today to stay at it until you achieve your dreams!

"Do things when they become difficult." — Unknown

You've heard the saying that failure is not an option. But since you know that failures are the building blocks of success—and the error feedback that helps you stay on target, let's change the saying to this.

"Giving up is not an option!"

The worst thing about giving up is that only God and the universe know just how close you might be to succeeding, to achieving your desire. What if you were only three feet from achieving your goal when you gave up? How would you feel then?

This is the tale of R.U. Darby as told by Napoleon Hill in the Classic "Think and Grow Rich".

"One of the most common cause of failure is the habit of quitting when one is overtaken by temporary defeat. Every person is guilty of this mistake at one time or another.

"R.U. Darby, who later became one of the most successful insurance salesmen in the country, tells the story of his uncle, who was caught by the 'gold fever' in the gold-rush days, and went west to dig and grow rich. He had never heard the saying that more gold has been mined from the brains of men than ever has been taken from the earth. He staked a claim and went to work with a pick and shovel. The going was hard, but his lust for gold was definite.

"After weeks of labor, he was rewarded by the discovery of the shining ore. He needed machinery to bring the ore to the surface. Quietly, he covered up the mine, retraced his footsteps to his home in Williamsburg, Maryland, and told his relatives and a few neighbors of the 'strike.' They got together money for the needed machinery and had it shipped. The Uncle and Darby went back to work the mine.

"The first car of ore was mined and shipped to a smelter. The returns proved they had one of the richest mines in Colorado! A few more cars of that ore would clear the debts. Then would come the big killing in profits.

"Down went the drills! Up went the hopes of Darby and Uncle! Then something happened—The vein of gold ore disappeared. They had come to the end of the rainbow, and the pot of gold was no longer there. They drilled on, desperately trying to pick up the vein again, all to no avail.

"Finally they decided to quit. They sold the machinery to a junk man for a few hundred dollars, and took the train back home. Some 'junk' men are dumb, but not this one! He called in a mining engineer to look at the mine and do a little calculating. The engineer advised that the project had failed because the others were not familiar with 'fault lines.' His calculations showed that the vein would be found *just three feet from where the Darbys had stopped drilling!* That is exactly where it was found.

"The junk man took millions of dollars in ore from the mine because he knew enough to seek expert council before giving up. Most of the money which went into the machinery was procured through the efforts of R.U. Darby, who was then a very young man. The money came from his relatives and neighbors, because of their faith in him. He paid back every dollar of it, although he was years in doing so.

"Long afterwards, Mr. Darby recouped his loss many times over when he made the discovery that desire can be transmuted into gold. The discovery came after he went into the business of selling life insurance.

"Remembering that he lost a huge fortune because he stopped three feet from gold, Darby profited by the experience in his chosen work. His simple method was to say to himself, 'I stopped three feet from gold, but I will never stop because men say "no" when I ask them to buy insurance.' He owes his 'stickability' to the lesson he learned from his 'quitibility' in the gold mining business."

Not only is this a perfect lesson about the importance of persistence, it is a golden example of what "learning from your failures" and "finding the good in every situation" can do for you. R.U. Darby could have faded in the pages of obscurity, the only footnote to his life being that he "stopped three feet from gold." Instead he used the lessons from the gold mining failure to propel him to incredible heights of financial success!

Are you going to stop three feet from gold?

Persistence is the result of faith, a clearly defined goal, purpose, desire, resilience, and habit.

Faith in self is important to persistence because when you believe you are capable of accomplishing your dream nothing can stop you. Faith that your goal is achievable is also critical to developing the passion you will need to succeed. Faith is the armor guarding your goal. Strong faith produces impenetrable armor. Weak faith produces armor that is ill fitting and leaves vital pieces of your goal unprotected.

A Clearly Defined Goal is critical to persistence because when you know exactly where you're going, you can plot your course over or around any obstacle. A clearly defined goal is the map and compass that guide you toward your destination. A poorly defined goal will lead you astray while a clearly defined goal will carry you through the most treacherous terrain.

Purpose is a key part of persistence because it isn't enough to know where you are going; you must also know why you are going there. Purpose is your steed on the path to your goal. Strong purpose will carry you tirelessly toward your destination. Weak or poorly developed purpose will try to stop and turn around at every opportunity.

Desire is an integral part of persistence because when you have strong desire, *you will find a way* to carry on during times of uncertainty. Desire is the nourishment for your dream. Because of this, desire and purpose are intricately linked. Weak desire will leave you with little endurance during times of difficulty. Strong desire will give you the energy you need to turn obstacles into opportunities.

Resilience is necessary to persistence because it allows you to adapt to new challenges and changing circumstances on the path to your goal. Resilience is the shield that allows you to deflect hazards when they unexpectedly appear before you. Strong resilience is fast and flexible and sidesteps many obstacles. Weak resilience may step right into an obstacle it is trying to avoid.

Habit is the bond that combines all of the parts of persistence into an unbreakable whole. Habit is the spell that makes you invincible on your quest. Strong habits produce consistent and positive results which continuously move you toward your goal. Weak habits produce haphazard movement in many directions and leave you vulnerable to anything that opposes you.

If you've struggled with persistence in the past, have heart! You can develop it. Start by setting smaller goals, things that you know you'll succeed at. Then follow through with them, no matter what. Make this a habit. When challenges arise—as they do with all goals—ask yourself, "What can I learn from this?" and "How can it help me?" Then use that information to strengthen your resolve and propel you toward the achievement of your goal.

Use Kaizen. Break your goal into smaller steps. Find the smallest step possible that when consistently executed will carry you to your goal. Then do it!

You'll find, as you create the habit of persistence, that your small steps will grow larger naturally. You will also discover that challenges are easier to overcome when you consistently ask the above questions.

As you follow the steps above, each success will build upon the last. The persistence you develop will become habit. And you will find yourself naturally applying this habit to the major goals in your life.

Challenge:
Make a small daily goal right now. Use something that will carry you toward one of your major goals. Commit Now to doing this action every day! If something happens that tries to interfere with your daily goal, find a way to turn it to your advantage by asking these questions, "What can I learn from this?" and "How can it help me?" And above all else, complete your daily goal!

When you do this, you'll not only develop the habit of persistence, you'll develop faith in yourself! And you will follow through on your commitments.

Key Points
> ***Carry on*** despite all obstacles and you will succeed!
> ***Strong persistence*** is built on these parts:
>> o   Faith
>> o   A Clearly defined goal
>> o   Purpose
>> o   Desire
>> o   Resilience
>> o   Habit
> ***Persistence can*** be developed. Start small and use persistence to create success. In a short time you'll start using the new found power of persistence in all areas of your life!

The final question is...

Where Do You Go From Here?

Achieving true success and fulfilling your desires and dreams is a journey. Reading this book and following the steps I've outlined are giant strides on the road toward your true destiny. The knowledge you've gained from this book is designed to help you find your true north and navigate to the realization of your dreams.

Everything you have done, every habit you've created while reading this book has opened up new opportunities for growth, change, and knowledge.

Seize these opportunities!

Following the steps and processes in this book *will produce* incredible changes in your life. You just have to follow the steps, listen to and act on your inspirations, and *let change happen*!

That's really all there is to it.

Yes, I've asked you to perform some tasks. I've asked you to give yourself ten minutes a day—when you read and review *Your Blueprint* and accompanying goals. But this time is a gift!

It is *your gift to YOU!*

You are giving yourself the gift of a wonderful, successful future.

There is one more thing I would ask of you. As you absorb and use this knowledge to create the successful life you desire, please share it with others.

Be a Mentor!

Roland Byrd

Schedule Roland for Speaking Engagements.
Email Contact@YourNewBlueprint.com

Sign up for my email newsletter:
Http://www.YourNewBlueprint.com/SignUp.htm

Visit my Blog:
Http://www.RolandByrd.com

Appendix A: Big Picture Worksheets

Character

What do you desire most from life when it comes to your Character?
Write these things here:

_____

_____

_____

_____

_____

_____

_____

_____

_____

_____

_____

_____

_____

_____

_____

_____

_____

_____

_____

_____

_____

_____

_____

_____

_____

_____

_____

_____

_____

_____

_____

_____

_____

_____

_____

_____

_____

_____

_____

_____

_____

Communication

What do you desire most from life when it comes to your Communication skills?

Write these things here:

_____

_____

_____

_____

_____

_____

_____

_____

_____

_____

_____

_____

_____

_____

_____

_____

_____

_____

_____

_____

_____

_____

_____

_____

_____

_____

_____

_____

_____

_____

_____

Emotional

What do you desire most from life Emotionally?
Write these things here:

_____

_____

_____

_____

_____

_____

_____

_____

_____

_____

_____

_____

_____

_____

_____

_____

_____

_____

_____

_____

_____

_____

_____

_____

_____

_____

_____

_____

_____

_____

_____

_____

_____

Financial

What do you desire most from life Financially?
Write these things here:

_____
_____
_____
_____
_____
_____
_____
_____
_____
_____
_____
_____
_____
_____
_____
_____
_____
_____
_____
_____
_____
_____
_____
_____
_____
_____
_____
_____
_____
_____
_____
_____

Mind

What Mental skills or changes do you desire most from life?
Write them here:

_____
_____
_____
_____
_____
_____
_____
_____
_____
_____
_____
_____
_____
_____
_____
_____
_____
_____
_____
_____
_____
_____
_____
_____
_____
_____
_____
_____
_____
_____
_____
_____
_____
_____
_____
_____

Physical

What do you desire most from life Physically? (Meaning from your Body
or something you do with your body.)
Write these things here:

_____

_____

_____

_____

_____

_____

_____

_____

_____

_____

_____

_____

_____

_____

_____

_____

_____

_____

_____

_____

_____

_____

_____

_____

_____

_____

_____

Spiritual

What do you desire most from life Spiritually?
Write these things here:

_____

_____

_____

_____

_____

_____

_____

_____

_____

_____

_____

_____

_____

_____

_____

_____

_____

_____

_____

_____

_____

_____

_____

_____

_____

_____

_____

_____

_____

_____

_____

_____

Appendix B: Traits List Worksheets

Character

What are the Character Traits you will need to achieve all of the desires
you listed on the Character *Big Picture Worksheet*?
Write them
here:_____

_____
_____
_____
_____
_____
_____
_____
_____
_____
_____
_____
_____
_____
_____
_____
_____
_____
_____
_____
_____
_____
_____
_____
_____
_____
_____
_____
_____
_____
_____
_____
_____
_____
_____
_____
_____
_____

Communication

What are the Communication Traits or skills you will need to achieve all of the desires you listed on the Communication *Big Picture Worksheet*?
Write them here:

_____

_____

_____

_____

_____

_____

_____

_____

_____

_____

_____

_____

_____

_____

_____

_____

_____

_____

_____

_____

_____

_____

_____

_____

_____

_____

_____

_____

_____

_____

_____

_____

_____

_____

Emotional

What are the Emotional Traits you will need to achieve all of the desires
you listed on the Emotional *Big Picture Worksheet*?
Write them here:

_____

_____

_____

_____

_____

_____

_____

_____

_____

_____

_____

_____

_____

_____

_____

_____

_____

_____

_____

_____

_____

_____

_____

_____

_____

_____

_____

_____

_____

_____

_____

_____

_____

_____

_____

_____

Financial

What are the Financial Traits or habits you will need to achieve all of the desires you listed on the Financial *Big Picture Worksheet*?
Write these things here:

_____
_____
_____
_____
_____
_____
_____
_____
_____
_____
_____
_____
_____
_____
_____
_____
_____
_____
_____
_____
_____
_____
_____
_____
_____
_____
_____
_____
_____
_____
_____
_____

Mental

What are the Mental Traits, habits, or processes you will need to achieve all of the desires you listed on the Mental *Big Picture Worksheet*?
Write them here:

_____

_____

_____

_____

_____

_____

_____

_____

_____

_____

_____

_____

_____

_____

_____

_____

_____

_____

_____

_____

_____

_____

_____

_____

_____

_____

_____

_____

_____

_____

_____

_____

_____

_____

Physical

What are the Physical Traits or habits you will need to achieve all of the desires you listed on the Physical *Big Picture Worksheet*?
Write these things here:

_____

_____

_____

_____

_____

_____

_____

_____

_____

_____

_____

_____

_____

_____

_____

_____

_____

_____

_____

_____

_____

_____

_____

_____

_____

_____

_____

_____

_____

_____

_____

Spiritual

What are the Spiritual Traits you will need to achieve all of the desires you listed on the Spiritual *Big Picture Worksheet*?
List them here:

_____

_____

_____

_____

_____

_____

_____

_____

_____

_____

_____

_____

_____

_____

_____

_____

_____

_____

_____

_____

_____

_____

_____

_____

_____

_____

_____

_____

_____

_____

_____

_____

_____

_____

_____

_____

_____

_____

_____

_____

Appendix C: Recommended Books & Courses

Anthony Robbins: *Awaken the Giant Within*
                        Unlimited Power
                        Get The Edge – Home Study Course

Bruce H. Lipton: *The Biology of Belief*

Deepak Chopra: *The Spontaneous Fulfillment of Desire*
                        Creating Affluence

Denis Waitley: *10 Seeds of Greatness*
                        Being the Best
                        Empires of the Mind

Douglas Scott Nelson: *Catch Fire*

Joe Vitale: *Attractor Factor*
                        Hypnotic Writing

John Medina: *Brain Rules*

Joseph Murphy: *The Power of Your Subconscious Mind*

Judith Orloff: *Second Sight*

Leslie Householder: *The Jackrabbit Factor*

Maxwell Maltz: *Psycho-Cybernetics*

Michael J. Gelb: *Discover Your Genius*

Michael J. Losier: *Law of Attraction*

Napoleon Hill: *Think and Grow Rich*
                        The Master Key to Riches

Patrick Combs: *Gearing Up*
                        Major in Success

Stephen R. Covey: *The 7 Habits of Highly Effective People*

Sean Stephenson: *Get Off Your "But"*

T. Harv Eker: *Secrets of the Millionaire Mind*
Millionaire Mind Intensive – 3 day seminar
*I was so impressed with this seminar that I decided to help promote it. If **you'd like to learn how you can get free tickets** to this amazing 3 day event, click the link below (Kindle) or enter it in the address bar of your Internet browser.*
http://bit.ly/MillionaireMindSeminar

Appendix D: Original Introduction

I've felt I needed to change the introduction to Your Blueprint, Life by Design for a while. With the original intro—below—I tried to give a glimpse of what my life was like before I learned to reprogram my subconscious mind.

I was a dark person. So the old intro feels dark. Perhaps that's not the best way to start a personal development book. I think it scared off some people who could have gained a lot from this book if they'd stuck around. I'm sorry for that.

I revised the intro to what you read in the front of the book today.

The original intro is here for those who want to understand the true depth of change the processes in this book created in my life—and in the lives of those near me.

It's not a lighthearted journey. *You are warned.*

My Journey from darkness—how the principles in this book changed my life.

My hands shook. Tears streamed down my face. The muzzle of the .22 rifle was cold and bitter in my mouth. I wanted to pull the trigger. The rifle was cocked and loaded. But I couldn't do it. For an eternity I sat there on the basement floor of my father's house, willing myself to get it over with, to end the pain once and for all. And still I sat, a statue of agony as all the sorrows of my life flowed from my eyes. I was more terrified of death than I was of living. I was a coward trapped between two immovable desires; Life and misery or Death and—as I believed then— ceasing to exist. I didn't know how to go on but I didn't know how to pull the trigger either. I knew that tonight was the night. I had to end it for good.

And then the thoughts entered my mind. *It has to get better someday! You are not a quitter!*

That was the first time in years I'd felt real hope. I was eighteen.

In time I removed the muzzle from my mouth and placed the gun on the floor. I called my best friend and asked him to come over and hide my rifle. When he got there he disassembled it and hid the pieces in different parts of the house. Then I cried on his shoulder for a while, a bizarre mixture of regret and relief coursing through me.

I've never touched that rifle again. I never even saw it again.

As I said, that was the first time in many years that I'd felt real hope. I'd like to say that was *the* turning point in my life, the time that changed everything.

It wasn't. That came later.

But it was a turning point.

The memory of those thoughts kept me alive during the bouts of depression I had in the years to come. Later they kept me from jumping from the roofs of the skyscrapers in Denver and Chicago—where I cleaned windows while in my twenties. In my early thirties, they kept me from leaping from the seventh floor of the parking garage on the days I worked in the office at my Network Engineering job. The memory of those thoughts weren't enough to stop the urge though. The urge to hurt myself, to end my life was always there in those situations.

The day *the urge disappeared* was the day I learned I could take control of my life, that I could *choose a better life*. It was the day my eyes began opening to the miraculous power of my mind. It was the day that I said, "*Enough*!" and finally meant it.

But why did I struggle so during those long cold years? Why was I severely depressed? Why were my relationships in shambles? Why was I always in emotional lockdown? Why did I perpetuate the harmful behaviors I'd learned as a child?

Those patterns and beliefs were fixed in my subconscious mind. They were my Blueprint. And like so many people in our world, I didn't know I could change it.

Flash back to a more innocent time.

I always wanted to be a hero. Even as a young child I knew I wanted to make a difference. With that came dreams of glory and grandeur. I imagined I would somehow gain superpowers and save the world. I would be someone that many, many people looked up to and respected. I would do something wonderful and leave a giant footprint on the sands of time.

I remember once when I was five... I walked around the front yard of the sagging, ranch style house we were vacating. (Just one in a series of what felt like hundreds of moves my family made while I was a child.) My path cut a giant figure eight in the lawn. I sang a song of hope and love. I don't recall the words now, but the feeling is still there. It lives on in my heart. I sang about being a hero and saving people. I sang about serving my country. I sang about noble sacrifices.

While I sang I held visions in my mind of rescuing people in times of peril. I believed I was capable of miracles and I basked in that knowledge.

But life happens. And though my desire to be a hero never died, my knowledge, my belief in my ability to make a difference waned. It faded until it was the smoky remnant of a long lost dream.

While I grew I experienced many things that I unconsciously allowed to chip away at the bright, shining belief I had in my abilities when I was a child. I learned damaging beliefs and behaviors from people I trusted and loved. (Unknown to me, these beliefs and behavioral patterns were safely tucked away in my subconscious mind. There they waited for the right conditions to manifest.)

By the time I was a teenager I'd bought into the popular stereotypes of the haunted hero—the man who did great things but was plagued by powerful demons from his past. I internalized this ideal and carried it into my adulthood.

I had my ups and my downs. I struggled with addictive behavior. I had times of emotional and spiritual clarity and times when I felt lost in the darkness. But even though my belief in my ability to do something good and help others had long ago diminished, I still felt called to do something, to make a difference. I just didn't know how.

And then came the day I awoke to discover I'd become the villain. I stared in the face of a man I didn't recognize. A man I loathed. I wondered why I hadn't just pulled the trigger that night so long ago. But it was too late for that now. No matter how much I wanted to die, I knew I couldn't do it. And I hated myself for that weakness.

Where was the hero I'd dreamt I'd become? What happened to the small child who wanted desperately to help others? Where had I gone wrong?

I had no answer to these questions...

Fast forward through misery.

I sat across the desk from a counselor who'd just finished explaining the "Cognitive Thinking Process" to me—you'll learn about this process later in the book. For the first time in my life I was taking conscious control of my thoughts.

I never knew I could do that.

I never knew I could choose the life I wanted. I'd wandered through life reacting to situation after situation—often with disastrous results. The concept of personal accountability was alien to me. But it felt right and I ran with it.

Since then I've never stopped running, moving ahead, recreating myself.

The man who wrote this today is as different from the man of misery as the man of misery was different from the child of hope. Who I am today is the result of years of deliberate change and growth. The man I am today is a product of a true desire to change and the willingness to do whatever it takes to make it happen. The man I am today is a student of life and hope and love and joy. The man I am today is a miracle, just like *you are a miracle!*

Your Blueprint, Life by Design is the culmination of years of change and growth. These changes were sometimes painful, looking in the mirror of your life often is, but they were always worth it!

I discovered that subconscious beliefs are largely responsible for the results we get in life. I call these beliefs *Your Blueprint.* Think of them as the autopilot that engages when you aren't consciously controlling your life—which is most of the time for many people. Or perhaps the image of a burly co-pilot who insists on going a different direction than what you desire is better. You can fight and fight your co-pilot, but he's a lot stronger than you (80% to 90% stronger) and in the end you'll lose the battle.

Imagine my surprise when I learned I could reprogram my Blueprint, that I could make my Blueprint my partner in success.

You can *reprogram Your Blueprint*!

Where force fails, you can talk sense into your co-pilot. He listens to reason. But *You have to convince him first.* Then he'll agree to fly toward the destination of your dreams instead of the destination he wants.

I learned to *cast aside the old beliefs and behavioral patterns* that came from living life as the victim of my history. *I programmed my subconscious mind with new, empowering beliefs and behavioral patterns.* I recreated the person I was and started to become the person I always knew I should be.

Once your co-pilot understands that what you want and what he wants are the same, your life will fly to heights of joy and happiness you've only imagined before.

I rewrote my Blueprint and in a short time I realized the results I was getting from life were aligning with my goals and dreams!

Why?

For the first time in my life my subconscious beliefs aligned with my desires.

I became one of the heroes of my life.

I challenge you to do the same. *Become a hero* of your life!

I believe the greatest thing about being human is our ability to take charge of our lives. Accept accountability today. Realize that, though your subconscious beliefs steer your life, *you control those beliefs.*

My true desire is to give you a platform you will use to *burst free of your cocoon*, to *realize your true inner power*, to *take control of your life* and *become the magnificent person you want to be* in all areas of your life.

Make the choice today, change your life, *change Your Blueprint!*

You *are* the master of your Destiny!

Roland

Made in the USA
Charleston, SC
03 January 2015